LIVE EVENTS

PROMOTIONAL GRAPHICS

ROCKPORT PUBLISHERS, INC. • ROCKPORT, MASSACHUSETTS
DISTRIBUTED BY NORTH LIGHT BOOKS, CINCINNATI, OHIO

DESIGN AND LAYOUT
Sara Day

EDITOR
Jim Cowen

PRODUCTION MANAGER
Barbara States

PRODUCTION ASSITANT
Pat O'Maley

ADDITIONAL PHOTOGRAPHY
Kevin Thomas

First Published in the United States of America by:
Rockport Publishers, Inc.
146 Granite Street
Rockport, MA 01966
Telephone: 508-546-9590
Fax: 508-546-7141

CONTENTS

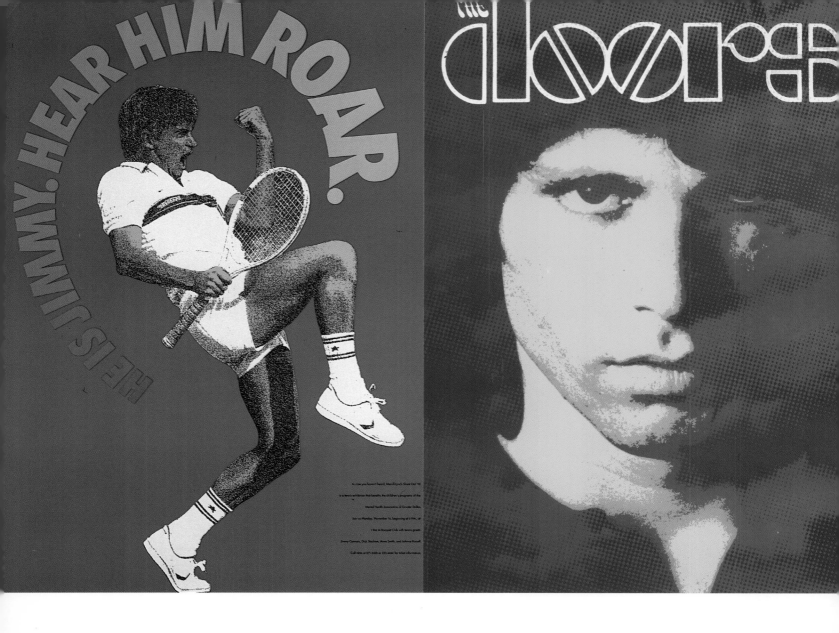

Live events are virtually any gathering intended to bring people together for a shared experience. Since 1970, billions of dollars have been spent constructing entertainment and sports palaces, a testimony that live events are big business! Live events prosper internationally, too, as trade fairs, art festivals, and meets such as the Olympics are organized worldwide. Superstars, tournaments, conventions and seminars criss-cross the nation daily, invading regional markets for a piece of the ticket pie. An impressive number of cities also support local talent; from teams to theatrical repertory, from

symphonic orchestras to opera and ballet. Each year, countless events spend millions promoting ticket sales to pack the venues. *Live Events* offers a comprehensive view of some of the best in contemporary graphics—proven designs that fill the seats.

This innovative collection features integrated design elements from "live" promotions. All aspects of promotional campaigns are included: posters, print ads, direct mail, invitations, brochures, and fliers, grouped to underscore the design continuity between campaign and merchandise. Artwork gathered from top designers, illustrators, and photographers from

around the world is presented here in beautiful, full-color. This is the perfect visual source book for event graphic designers and promoters, with categories covering Performing Arts events, Museums, Galleries and Exhibitions, Fund Raisers, Sporting, and Corporate events, plus many more.

For sheer impact and artistic presence, the poster has long been a designer favorite—hence the overwhelming response. Posters enhance the importance of an event, says Dave Bartels of Bartels & Company in St. Louis. "For their economy, they really set a mood. Posters can be magical!" says Bartels, "A great format to

INTRODUCTION

celebrate, commemorate and announce events!" Illustrator Bill Nelson reports that, recently, the calibre of poster design, graphics, illustration, and photography has improved by leaps and bounds. "Everybody seems to want something really classy and beautiful now, " says Nelson. "I applaud it!"

The Pushpin Group's Seymour Chwast agrees; "Posters are grand. Their size demands attention. They compete with fine art in museums. Artist Gary Ciccarelli's festival poster for Montreaux Jazz Detroit (p.15) is considered just that—though now out of print, the poster has become a legendary collectable.

The Bronx Zoo's startling Shark and Hippo subway posters (p.74) were designed to attract visitors, but did their job too well—they were dubbed "the most stolen" posters in the MTA's history. John Muller's poster design for the Kansas City Jazz Pub Crawl is another great commentary on just how desperate people can be to own an outstanding poster. "People just went crazy, " says Muller, "trying to grab them off the walls."

As mementos, posters—like T-shirts—can pay their way. Winterland Productions' Troy Alders, an art director with accounts like Madonna and Hammer, sells thousands. Rick Vaughn of

Vaughn/Wedeen Creative routinely orders five hundred silk-screened posters to offer for sale along with 5,000 T-shirts for the annual Duke City Marathon. John Sayles, an event graphics specialist, puts it succinctly: Posters are great fun!

Live Events Promotional Graphics comes alive with posters on nearly every page, plus special designs for tickets, and a vivid collection of collateral and novelty items.

—Jim Cowen

Compiled in conjunction with Rockport Publishers by Jim Cowen, Illustrator/Art Director for *Next Door Productions*, and Event Promotions Director for *Performance Magazine, the International Touring Talent Weekly.*

Event UCSD Jazz Festival
Description of Piece(s) Poster
Design Firm University Events Office, UC San Diego
Art Director Ruth Baily
Designer Ruth Baily
Illustrator Ruth Baily

A mix of forties geometrics and nineties colors reflect Jazz Festival favorite Charlie Haden, a veteren of the late 1940s and early 1950s jazz scene.

Event Budweiser Jazz and Rib Fest
Description of Piece(s) Poster
Design Firm Rickabaugh Graphics
Art Director Eric Rickabaugh
Designer Mark Krumel

The poster ties in with banners, T-shirts, and bus signs.

EVENT MONTREUX JAZZ DETROIT
DESIGN FIRM BRADLEY, GELMAN ASSOCIATES, INC.
ILLUSTRATOR GARY CICCARELLI

EVENT PLAYBOX PROMOTIONS
DESCRIPTION OF PIECE(S) THEATRE COMPANY BROCHURE
DESIGN FIRM CATO DESIGN INC.
DESIGNER NIGEL BEECHEY
THEATRE COMPANY

EVENT LENNY HENRY LOUDI AUTUMN TOUR
DESCRIPTION OF PIECE(S) BROCHURE, T-SHIRT
DESIGN FIRM THE GREEN HOUSE
ART DIRECTOR JUDI GREEN
DESIGNER JUDI GREEN, JAMES BELL
PHOTOGRAPHER TREVOR LEIGHTON

EVENT 10TH ANNIVERSARY OF VICTORIAN
ARTS CENTRE
DESCRIPTION OF PIECE(S) POSTER, BANNERS
DESIGN FIRM CATO DESIGN INC.
DESIGNER KEN CATO

11

EVENT 11TH SEATTLE INTERNATIONAL FILM FESTIVAL
DESCRIPTION OF PIECE(S) POSTER
TYPE DESIGNER BRUCE HALE
ILLUSTRATOR STEPHEN PERINGER

EVENT "JAZZ LIVE AT THE HYATT"
DESCRIPTION OF PIECE(S) POSTER
DESIGN FIRM SAYLES GRAPHIC DESIGN
ART DIRECTOR JOHN SAYLES
DESIGNER JOHN SAYLES

THIS POSTER PROMOTES A SUMMER JAZZ SERIES.

EVENT NOCHES DE JAZZ HEINEKEN
    HEINEKEN JAZZFEST
DESCRIPTION OF PIECE(S) POSTERS, COASTER, PLAYBILL
DESIGN FIRM C.O.W. CREATIVE OPERATIONS WORKSHOP
ART DIRECTOR DENNIS LOPEZ-LUNA
DESIGNER DENNIS LOPEZ-LUNA
ILLUSTRATOR DENNIS LOPEZ-LUNA

HEINEKEN SPONSORS THIS SERIES OF JAZZ CONCERTS
THROUGHOUT THE ISLAND.

CLOCKWISE FROM TOP LEFT

Event B 52's
Description of Piece(s) Poster

Description of Piece(s) Hammer
Design Firm Winterland Productions
Art Director Sandra Horvat Vallely
Designer Colin Birdseye
Photographer Annie Leibovitz

Event Live Pilot Presentation
Design Firm Nancy Stutman Calligraphics
Art Director John O'Melveny Woods
Calligrapher Nancy Stutman

This project, a Saturday Night Live–type pilot for teenagers was primarily for television executives and production heads.

EVENT PALM SPRINGS INTERNATIONAL FILM FESTIVAL
DESCRIPTION OF PIECE(S) POSTER, PROGRAM COVER,
TICKETS, TICKET ORDER FORM, APPAREL, STATIONERY
DESIGN FIRM MARK PALMER DESIGN
ART DIRECTOR MARK PALMER
DESIGNER MARK PALMER
ILLUSTRATOR MARK PALMER, CURTIS PALMER

CLOCKWISE FROM TOP LEFT

EVENT BB KING WORLD TOUR
DESCRIPTION OF PIECE(S) POSTER
DESIGN FIRM NEXT DOOR PRODUCTIONS
ART DIRECTOR JIM COWEN
DESIGNER JIM COWEN
ILLUSTRATOR JIM COWEN

PORTRAIT WAS ALSO A MAGAZINE COVER AND AD, POSTCARD, AND THE FACE OF A PROMOTIONAL WATCH.

EVENT HOUSTON SYMPHONY
DESCRIPTION OF PIECE(S) POSTER
DESIGN FIRM METROPOLIS, INC.
ART DIRECTOR DENISE MENDELSOHN
DESIGNER LISA MARIE DE SENO

EVENT KC BLUES AND JAZZ FESTIVAL
DESCRIPTION OF PIECE(S) T-SHIRT
DESIGN FIRM WRK DESIGN
ART DIRECTOR ANN WILLOUGHBY
ILLUSTRATOR ANN WILLOUGHBY

EVENT HYDE IN HOLLYWOOD
DESCRIPTION OF PIECE(S) POSTER
DESIGN FIRM JOHN JINX STUDIO

EVENT "THE MAGIC FLUTE"/OPERA SEASON
DESCRIPTION OF PIECE(S) POSTER
DESIGN FIRM MAY & CO.
ILLUSTRATOR GARY OVERACRE

Event Club Hubelin
Description of Piece(s) Poster
Design Firm John Jinx Studio

EVENT Fremont Fair
DESCRIPTION OF PIECE(S) Poster
DESIGN FIRM Modern Dog
ART DIRECTOR Vittorio Costarella, Al Parisi
DESIGNER Vittorio Costarella
ILLUSTRATOR Vittorio Costarella

This illustration was depicting the celebration of the summer solstice through music, art, and theatre, done at 100% using arcylics and colored pencils.

EVENT Capa Signature
Classical Concerts Series
DESCRIPTION OF PIECE(S) Brochure
DESIGN FIRM Rickabaugh Graphics
ART DIRECTOR Eric Rickabaugh
DESIGNER Tina Zientarski
ILLUSTRATOR Eric Rickabaugh

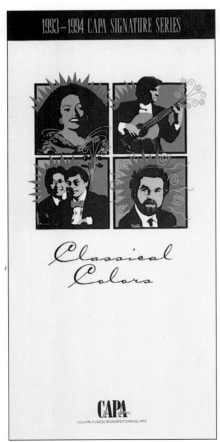

MUSIC
IN
THE
AIR

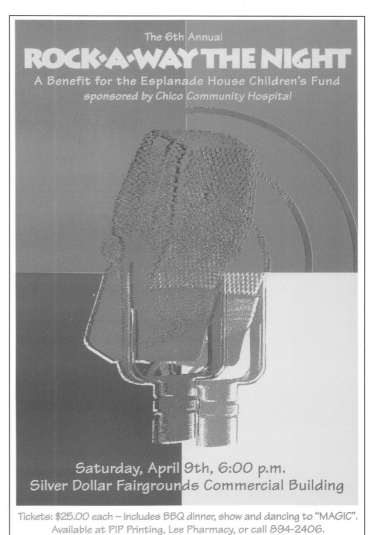

The 6th Annual

ROCK·A·WAY THE NIGHT

A Benefit for the Esplanade House Children's Fund
sponsored by Chico Community Hospital

Saturday, April 9th, 6:00 p.m.
Silver Dollar Fairgrounds Commercial Building

Tickets: $25.00 each – includes BBQ dinner, show and dancing to "MAGIC".
Available at PIP Printing, Lee Pharmacy, or call 894-2406.

CLOCKWISE FROM TOP LEFT

EVENT MUSIC IN THE AIR CONCERTS
DESCRIPTION OF PIECE(S) POSTER
DESIGN FIRM RICKABAUGH GRAPHICS
ART DIRECTOR ERIC RICKABAUGH
DESIGNER ERIC RICKABAUGH
ILLUSTRATOR ERIC RICKABAUGH

THIS POSTER WAS CREATED ENTIRELY IN ALDUS FREEHAND.

EVENT ROCK A WAY THE NIGHT BENEFIT
DESCRIPTION OF PIECE(S) POSTER
DESIGN FIRM IMAGE GROUP
ART DIRECTOR DAN FRAZIER
DESIGNER DAN FRAZIER, CHRISTINE BROCKMAN
ILLUSTRATOR DAN FRAZIER, CHRISTINE BROCKMAN

EVENT CONCERT FOR PEACE
PENN STATE GLEE CLUB PERFORMANCE
DESCRIPTION OF PIECE(S) POSTER (OFFSET)
DESIGN FIRM SOMMESE DESIGN
ART DIRECTOR LANNY SOMMESE
DESIGNER LANNY SOMMESE
ILLUSTRATOR LANNY SOMMESE

CONCERT
FOR
PEACE

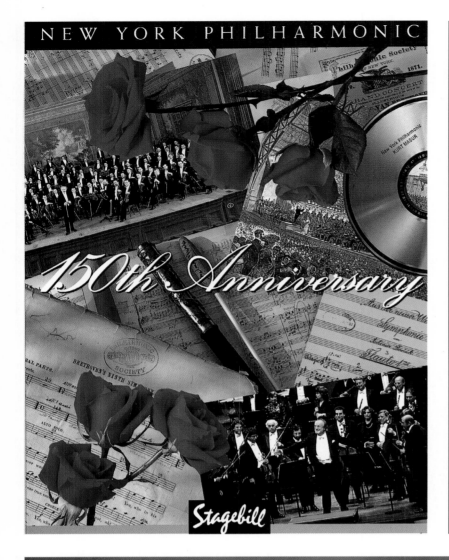

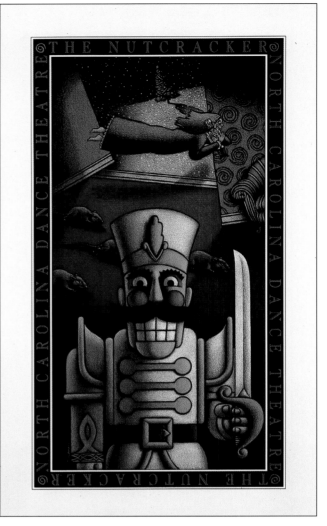

EVENT John Trudell Spoken Word Tour
DESCRIPTION OF PIECE(S) Poster
DESIGN FIRM Gary Houston Design
ART DIRECTOR Gary Houston
DESIGNER Gary Houston
ILLUSTRATOR Gary Houston

EVENT Verdi/Rigoletto
DESIGN FIRM Takayuki Ito Design Office
ART DIRECTOR Takayuki Ito
DESIGNER Masayuki Tsukamoto
ILLUSTRATOR Takayuki Ito

Event Led Zeppelin
Description of Piece(s) Poster
Design Firm Winterland Productions
Art Director Sandra Horvat Vallely
Designer Bryan Berry
Photographer Bob Gruen

Event Niggaz 4 N.W.A.
Description of Piece(s) Poster

EVENT SOUND GARDEN TOUR
DESCRIPTION OF PIECE(S) POSTER
ART DIRECTOR CATHY CLEGHORN
DESIGNER RICHARD NELSON
PHOTOGRAPHER KRISTIN CALLAHAN,
LANCE MERRER

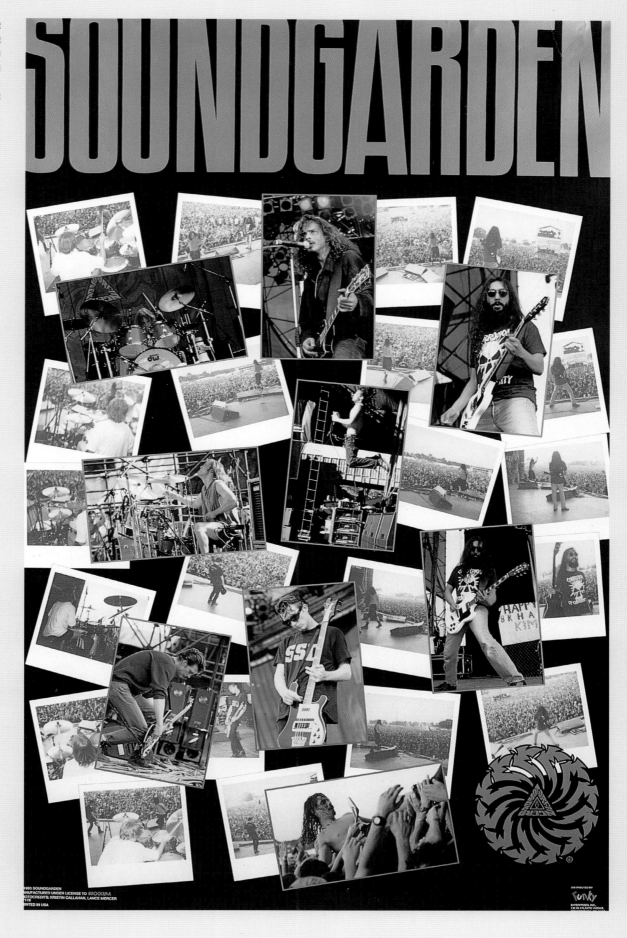

EVENT JERRY GARCIA BAND TOUR
DESCRIPTION OF PIECE(S) AIRBRUSH AND ACRYLIC
    POSTERS, T-SHIRTS
DESIGN FIRM HAPPYLIFE PRODUCTIONS
ART DIRECTOR MICHAEL DUBOIS
DESIGNER MICHAEL DUBOIS
ILLUSTRATOR MICHAEL DUBOIS
PHOTOGRAPHER STORM PHOTO

EVENT ALLMAN BROTHERS TOUR
DESCRIPTION OF PIECE(S) ACRYLIC AND AIRBRUSH
DESIGN FIRM HAPPYLIFE PRODUCTIONS
ART DIRECTOR MICHAEL DUBOIS
DESIGNER MICHAEL DUBOIS
ILLUSTRATOR MICHAEL DUBOIS
PHOTOGRAPHER STORM PHOTO

USED FOR CONCERT T-SHIRTS AND PROJECTION ON
STAGE BACKDROP.

EVENT GRATEFUL DEAD SPRING TOUR
DESCRIPTION OF PIECE(S) AIRBRUSH AND MIXED MEDIA
    T-SHIRTS
DESIGN FIRM HAPPYLIFE PRODUCTIONS
ART DIRECTOR MICHAEL DUBOIS
DESIGNER MICHAEL DUBOIS
ILLUSTRATOR MICHAEL DUBOIS
PHOTOGRAPHER STORM PHOTO

USED FOR A 15 CITY U.S. TOUR PROMOTION

EVENT CINCINNATI BALLET
DESCRIPTION OF PIECE(S) SEASON
MINI POSTERS
DESIGN FIRM CATT LYON DESIGN INC.
ART DIRECTOR CHARLENE CATT LYON
DESIGNER CHARLENE CATT LYON
ILLUSTRATOR ALAN KASTNER

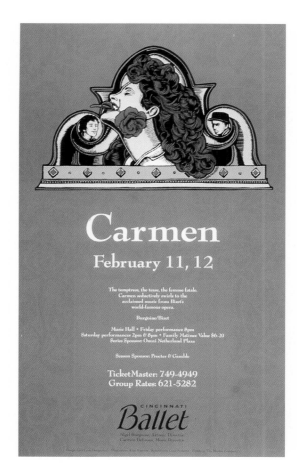

Carmen

February 11, 12

The temptress, the tease, the femme fatale.
Carmen seductively swirls to the
acclaimed music from Bizet's
world-famous opera.

Burgoine/Bizet

Music Hall • Friday performance 8pm
Saturday performances 2pm & 8pm • Family Matinee Value $6-20
Series Sponsor: Omni Netherland Plaza

Season Sponsor: Procter & Gamble

TicketMaster: 749-4949
Group Rates: 621-5282

CINCINNATI
Ballet
Nigel Burgoine, Artistic Director
Carmon DeLeone, Music Director

The Sleeping Beauty

October 22, 23, 24

Awaken your senses and relive the magical
tale of the sleeping princess.
Burgoine/Tchaikovsky
Music Hall • Friday performance 8pm
Saturday performances 2pm & 8pm
Sunday performance 2pm • Family Matinee Value $6-20
Series Sponsor: Thompson, Hine and Flory
Season Sponsor: Procter & Gamble

TicketMaster: 749-4949
Group Rates: 621-5282

CINCINNATI
Ballet
Nigel Burgoine, Artistic Director
Carmon DeLeone, Music Director

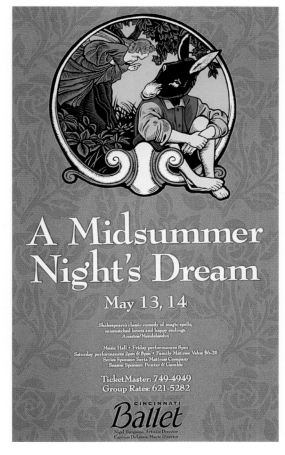

A Midsummer Night's Dream

May 13, 14

Shakespeare's classic comedy of magic spells,
mismatched lovers and happy endings.
Anastos/Mendelssohn

Music Hall • Friday performances 8pm
Saturday performances 2pm & 8pm • Family Matinee Value $6-20
Series Sponsor: Serta Mattress Company
Season Sponsor: Procter & Gamble

TicketMaster: 749-4949
Group Rates: 621-5282

CINCINNATI
Ballet
Nigel Burgoine, Artistic Director
Carmon DeLeone, Music Director

Spring Dance Festival

I. April 1, 2
Carmina Burana, Les Sylphides

II. April 29, 30
Rite of Spring, Agon, Serenade

Something for everyone!
A vivacious variety of one-act ballets.
Music Hall • Friday performances 8pm
Saturday performances 2pm & 8pm • Family Matinee Value $6-20
Series Sponsor: Renaissance Investment Council
Season Sponsor: Procter & Gamble

TicketMaster: 749-4949
Group Rates: 621-5282

CINCINNATI
Ballet
Nigel Burgoine, Artistic Director
Carmon DeLeone, Music Director

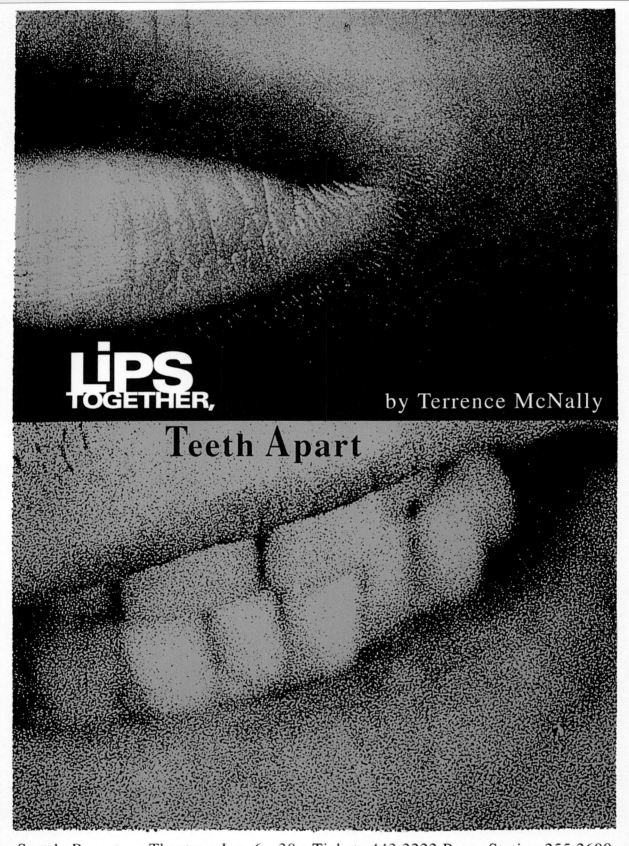

Seattle Repertory Theatre • Jan. 6 - 30 • Tickets 443.2222 PowerStation 255.2600

Poster by Modern Dog. Printing by Two Dimensions with water-based inks on recycled paper.

EVENT "LIPS TOGETHER, TEETH APART"/THEATRE
DESCRIPTION OF PIECE(S) POSTER
DESIGN FIRM MODERN DOG
ART DIRECTOR ROBYNNE RAYE, DOUGLAS HUGHES
DESIGNER ROBYNNE RAYE

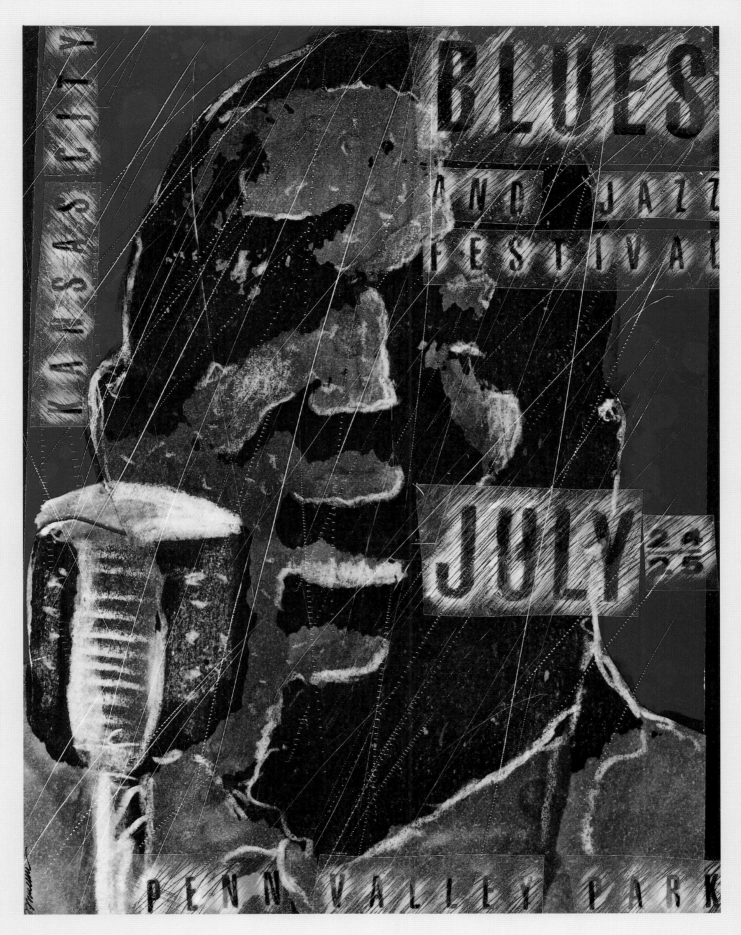

EVENT BLUES & JAZZ FEST
DESCRIPTION OF PIECE(S) POSTER
DESIGN FIRM MULLER + COMPANY
ART DIRECTOR JOHN MULLER
DESIGNER JOHN MULLER
ILLUSTRATOR JOHN MULLER

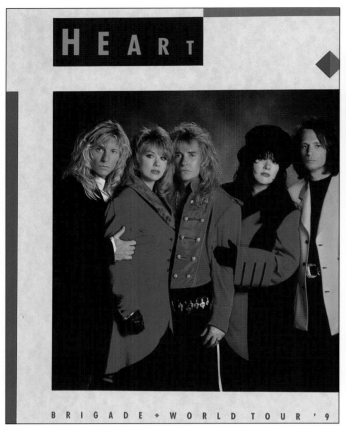

Event Heart Brigade World Tour/Heart Concert
Description of Piece(s) Tour book
Design Firm Design Art, Inc.
Art Director Norman Moore
Designer Norman Moore
Photographer Greg Gorman (front cover), Various

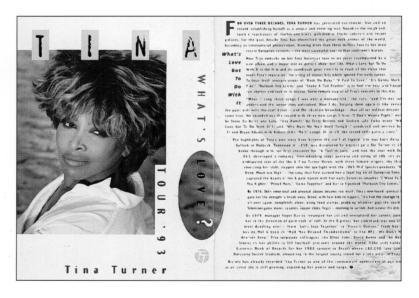

Event Tina "What's Love?" Tour/Tina Turner Concert
Description of Piece(s) Tour book
Design Firm Design Art, Inc.
Art Director Norman Moore
Designer Norman Moore, Chris Moore
Photographer Herb Ritts (front cover), Various

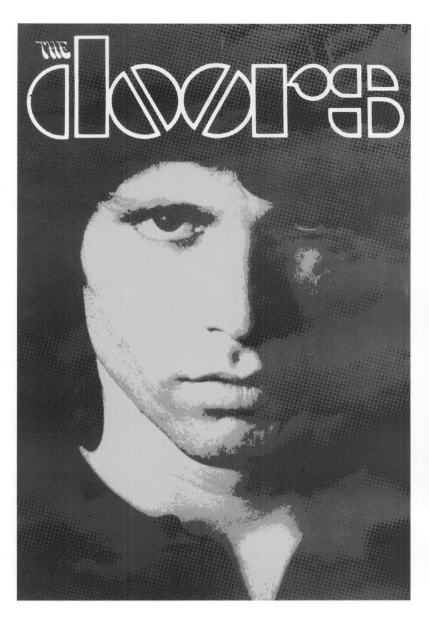

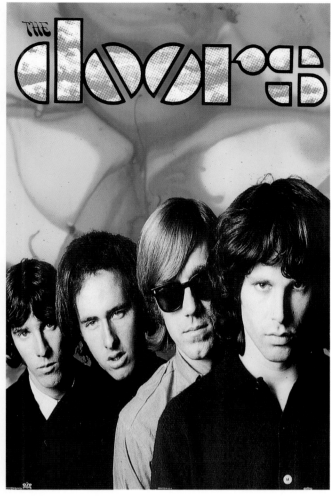

CLOCKWISE FROM TOP LEFT

EVENT JIM MORRISON
DESCRIPTION OF PIECE(S) POSTER
DESIGN FIRM WINTERLAND PRODUCTIONS
ART DIRECTOR TROY ALDERS
DESIGNER ANDREW SNIDER
PHOTOGRAPHER JOEL BRODSKY

DESCRIPTION OF PIECE(S) THE DOORS
DESIGN FIRM WINTERLAND PRODUCTIONS
ART DIRECTOR TROY ALDERS
DESIGNER ANDREW SNIDER

EVENT RINGO STARR CELEBRITY WEEKEND
DESCRIPTION OF PIECE(S) POSTER
DESIGN FIRM BOELTS BROS. DESIGN INC.
ART DIRECTOR JACKSON BOELTS, ERIC BOELTS
DESIGNER JACKSON BOELTS, ERIC BOELTS

DESIGN WAS DONE USING ALDUS FREEHAND.

EVENT PRIMUS
DESCRIPTION OF PIECE(S) POSTER
DESIGN FIRM WINTERLAND PRODUCTIONS
ART DIRECTOR TROY ALDERS
DESIGNER BRIAN CARROLL
PHOTOGRAPHER ANDREW MACNAUGHTON

DESCRIPTION OF PIECE(S) U2 ZOO TV
DESIGN FIRM WORKS ASSOCIATES
ART DIRECTOR STEVE AVERILL
DESIGNER SHAUGHN MCGRATY

EVENT NEIL YOUNG WITH BOOKER T AND THE MG'S
DESCRIPTION OF PIECE(S) POSTER
ART DIRECTOR CATHY CLAYBORN
DESIGNER REBECCA HOLLAND WITH LOVE
ILLUSTRATOR REBECCA HOLLAND WITH LOVE
PHOTOGRAPHER JOEL BERNSTEIN

DON GIOVANNI

BY WOLFGANG MOZART

November 16, 17, & 18 The Palace Theatre 8 p.m. ♥

Don Giovanni never misses a trick. Equally pleased by old or young, plain or ugly, thin or fat, he is a tomcat in satin breeches, a joker — and wild. He gambles everything for pleasure, defies convention, rebels against propriety. And, when he refuses to repent, he seals his fate in hell. Endless flirtations, little conspiracies, mistaken identities, and the supernatural fill Mozart's "jolly play," with the ultimate message . . . "in this life scoundrels always receive their just deserts." **A great season is in the cards!**

Sung in Italian with Opera/Titles in English

OPERA COLUMBUS

BORIS GODUNOV

BY MODEST MUSSORGSKY

March 22, 23, & 24 The Palace Theatre 8 p.m. ♣

Boris Godunov plays a fateful hand. By eliminating the competition, he stacks the deck in his favor, and ascends the throne of Russia. But his guilt poisons the gain. This epic drama bears the name of one man, but embraces the pageantry and pain of an aged Mother Russia. Inspired by the folk and liturgical idioms of his native land, Mussorgsky's lyrical score dramatically captures the strength and torment of the Russian soul. **A great season is in the cards!**

Sung in Russian with Opera/Titles in English

OPERA COLUMBUS

DESIGN: RICKABAUGH GRAPHICS • ART: MARK REIDY • PAPER: GILBERT® OXFORD, CINDER, 65 LB. COVER

DESIGN: RICKABAUGH GRAPHICS • ART: MARK REIDY • PAPER: GILBERT® OXFORD, TOAST, 80 LB. COVER

IL TROVATORE

BY GIUSEPPE VERDI

April 26, 27, & 28 The Palace Theatre 8 p.m. ♦

The gypsy holds all the cards. With deception and madness she fuels the destruction of a family. Her vengeance pits brother against brother in a tragic rivalry that can only end in death. Knights and troubadours, noblemen and gypsies abound in one of Verdi's most celebrated scores. With its thrilling melodies and rousing ensembles, Il Trovatore is a masterpiece of grand opera. **A great season is in the cards!**

Sung in Italian with Opera/Titles in English

OPERA COLUMBUS

CARMEN

BY GEORGES BIZET

October 12, 13, & 14 The Palace Theatre 8 p.m. ♠

Carmen's game is love. With bewitching insolence, she bullies the factory girls and tantalizes the townsfolk, to snare one lover after another. But she cannot win. When others find wealth and romance in the cards, she finds doom. In a magnificent and robust score — charged with such colorful music as the "Toreador's Song," "Habanera," and "Seguidilla" — Bizet creates the tale of a spitfire who plays the game of love passionately, courageously — to the very moment of her death. **A great season is in the cards!**

Sung in French with Opera/Titles in English

OPERA COLUMBUS

DESIGN: RICKABAUGH GRAPHICS • ART: MARK REIDY • PAPER: GILBERT® OXFORD, CINDER, 65 LB. COVER

DESIGN: RICKABAUGH GRAPHICS • ART: MARK REIDY • PAPER: GILBERT® OXFORD, CINDER, 65 LB. COVER

EVENT COLUMBUS OPERA SEASON
DESCRIPTION OF PIECE(S) POSTERS
DESIGN FIRM RICKABAUGH GRAPHICS
ART DIRECTOR ERIC RICKABAUGH
DESIGNER ERIC RICKABAUGH
ILLUSTRATOR MARK RIEDY

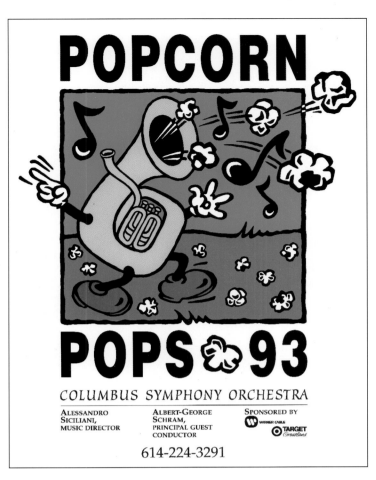

POPCORN

POPS ✿ 93

COLUMBUS SYMPHONY ORCHESTRA

ALESSANDRO
SICILIANI,
MUSIC DIRECTOR

ALBERT-GEORGE
SCHRAM,
PRINCIPAL GUEST
CONDUCTOR

SPONSORED BY

WARNER CABLE
TARGET Greatland

614-224-3291

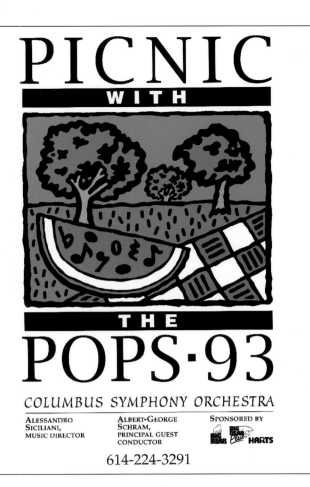

PICNIC

WITH

THE

POPS·93

COLUMBUS SYMPHONY ORCHESTRA

ALESSANDRO
SICILIANI,
MUSIC DIRECTOR

ALBERT-GEORGE
SCHRAM,
PRINCIPAL GUEST
CONDUCTOR

SPONSORED BY

BIG BEAR Blue HARTS

614-224-3291

CLOCKWISE FROM TOP LEFT

EVENT POPCORN POPS
DESCRIPTION OF PIECE(S) POSTER
DESIGN FIRM NEW IDEA DESIGN INC.
DESIGNER RON BOLDT
ILLUSTRATOR RON BOLDT

EVENT PICNIC WITH THE POPS
DESCRIPTION OF PIECE(S) POSTER
DESIGN FIRM NEW IDEA DESIGN INC.
DESIGNER RON BOLDT
ILLUSTRATOR RON BOLDT

EVENT "NUTCRACKER"/BALET WEST
DESCRIPTION OF PIECE(S) PROGRAM
DESIGN FIRM MILLS PUBLISHING/
RICHARDS & SWENSON
ART DIRECTOR NANI DIAZ
ILLUSTRATOR BILL SWENSON

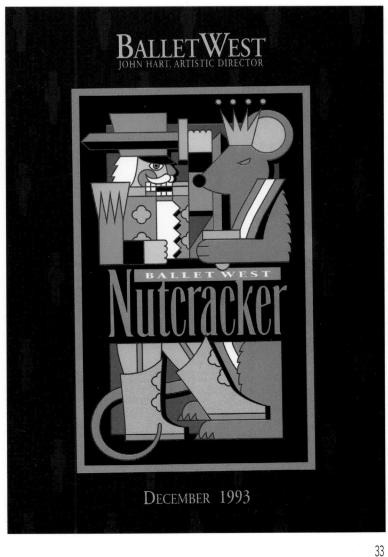

BALLET WEST
JOHN HART, ARTISTIC DIRECTOR

BALLET WEST
Nutcracker

DECEMBER 1993

DINOSAURISM

AN ILLUMINATED MANIFESTO

written by *John Allen Cann*
directed by *John Hostetter*

the players   Del Appleby
John Hostetter
John Allen Cann
Steve Hopkins
Gideon Davis

JUNE 6·7·8
THURSDAY TO SATURDAY
8:30 PM

OLIO THEATRE   3709 SUNSET BLVD.
(6 Blocks E. of Vermont)

Reservations: (213) 660-0729 / Tickets: $6.00

CLOCKWISE FROM TOP LEFT

EVENT LOLLIPOP CONCERT/COLUMBUS SYMPHONE ORCHESTRA
DESCRIPTION OF PIECE(S) ANNOUNCEMENTS
DESIGN FIRM NEW IDEA DESIGN INC.
DESIGNER RON BOLDT
ILLUSTRATOR RON BOLDT

KINGS, QUEENS AND DRAGONS MADE UP THIS SET OF
ANNOUNCEMENTS FOR A CHILDREN'S CONCERT BY THE
COLUMBUS SYMPHONY ORCHESTRA.

EVENT DINOSAURISM/A PLAY
DESCRIPTION OF PIECE(S) POSTER, PROGRAM
    (LETTERPRESS PRINTED)
DESIGN FIRM ADELE BASS & CO. DESIGN
ART DIRECTOR ADELE BASS
DESIGNER ADELE BASS
ILLUSTRATOR ADELE BASS

SOUND SHAPE & STYLE

EIGHTH AUSTRALIAN NATIONAL BAND AND ORCHESTRA CLINIC

A three day Conference featuring
International and Australian Clinicians
and Superb Concerts

FRIDAY JULY 1 TO SUNDAY JULY 3, 1994
PERTH MODERN SENIOR SCHOOL
PERTH, WESTERN AUSTRALIA

Presented by the
AUSTRALIAN BAND AND ORCHESTRA
DIRECTORS' ASSOCIATION

EVENT "CAROUSEL"/BROADWAY MUSICAL
DESCRIPTION OF PIECE(S) POSTER
DESIGN FIRM RUSSEK ADVERTISING, INC.
CREATIVE DIRECTOR JAMES RUSSEK
ILLUSTRATOR JAMES MCMULLAN

EVENT 8TH AUSTRALIAN NATIONAL BAND
AND ORCHESTRA CLINIC
DESCRIPTION OF PIECE(S) PROMOTIONAL
BROCHURE, REGISTRATION FORMS
DESIGN FIRM DILLON GRAPHICS
ART DIRECTOR SANDRA DILLON, DEBORAH MARIREA
DESIGNER SANDRA DILLON, DEBORAH MARIREA
ILLUSTRATOR DEBORAH MARIREA

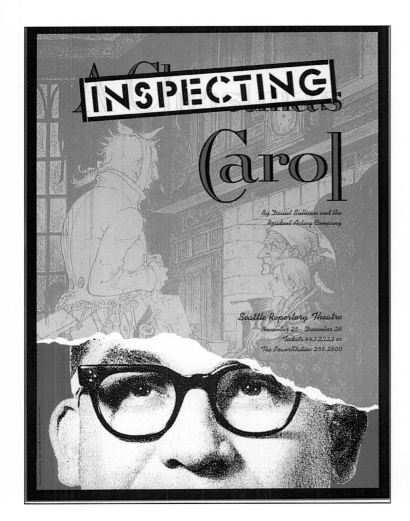

CLOCKWISE FROM TOP LEFT

EVENT "INSPECTING CAROL"/THEATRE
DESCRIPTION OF PIECE(S) POSTER
DESIGN FIRM MODERN DOG
ART DIRECTOR MICHAEL STRASSBURGER, DANIEL SULLIVAN
DESIGNER MICHAEL STRASSBURGER

EVENT "GREASE"/THEATRE
DESCRIPTION OF PIECE (S) POSTER
DESIGN FIRM MODERN DOG
ART DIRECTOR VITTORIO COSTARELLA,
    MICHAEL STASSBURGER
DESIGNER VITTORIO COSTARELLA, MICHAEL STRASSBURGER

EVENT "ZOOFARI BY THE SEA"/ANNUAL FUNDRAISER FOR
    COLUMBUS ZOO
DESCRIPTION OF PIECE(S) POSTER
DESIGN FIRM INTEGRATE, INC.
ART DIRECTOR DARRYL LEVERING
DESIGNER STEPHEN QUINN
ILLUSTRATOR DARRYL LEVERING

EVENT Humperdink/Hänsel und Gretel
DESIGN FIRM Takayuki Ito Design Office
ART DIRECTOR Takayuki Ito
DESIGNER Masayuki Tsukamoto
ILLUSTRATOR Takayuki Ito

EVENT Nutcracker/Ballet
DESIGN FIRM Takayuki Ito Design Office
ART DIRECTOR Takayuki Ito
DESIGNER Masayuki Tsukamoto
ILLUSTRATOR Takayuki Ito

EVENT Cincinnati Ballet
DESCRIPTION OF PIECE(S) Season Brochure
DESIGN FIRM Catt Lyon Design Inc.
ART DIRECTOR Charlene Catt Lyon
DESIGNER Charlene Catt Lyon, Hillary Middlekauf
ILLUSTRATOR Alan Kastner
PHOTOGRAPHER Alan Brown/Photonics Graphics

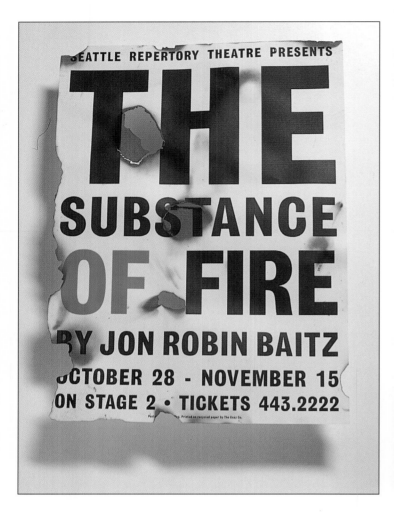

SEATTLE REPERTORY THEATRE PRESENTS

THE SUBSTANCE OF FIRE

BY JON ROBIN BAITZ

OCTOBER 28 - NOVEMBER 15
ON STAGE 2 • TICKETS 443.2222

SEATTLE REPERTORY THEATRE PRESENTS

EYE OF GOD

BY TIM BLAKE NELSON

STAGE 2 • JANUARY 27 - FEBRUARY 14, 1992 • TICKETS 443-2222

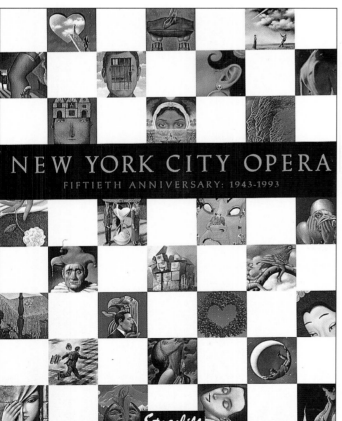

NEW YORK CITY OPERA

FIFTIETH ANNIVERSARY: 1943-1993

Stagebill

CLOCKWISE FROM TOP LEFT

EVENT "THE SUBSTANCE OF FIRE"/THEATRE
DESCRIPTION OF PIECE(S) POSTER (HAND-BURNED)
DESIGN FIRM MODERN DOG
ART DIRECTOR ROBYNNE RAYE, DOUGLAS HUGHES
DESIGNER ROBYNNE RAYE

EVENT "EYE OF GOD"/THEATRE
DESCRIPTION OF PIECE(S) POSTER
DESIGN FIRM MODERN DOG
ART DIRECTOR ROBYNNE RAYE, MICHAEL STRASSBURGER
DESIGNER ROBYNNE RAYE, MICHAEL STRASSBURGER
ILLUSTRATOR MICHAEL STRASSBURGER

EVENT NEW YORK CITY OPERA 50TH ANNIVERSARY
DESCRIPTION OF PIECE(S) SOUVENIR BOOK
DESIGN FIRM STAGEBILL
ART DIRECTOR ALEX STARK
DESIGNER ALEX STARK

Belinda

"Good Heavens!" WORLD TOUR

BELINDA CARLISLE

RUNAWAY HORSES WORLD TOUR 1990

CLOCKWISE FROM TOP LEFT

EVENT BELINDA "GOOD HEAVENS!"
WORLD TOUR/BELINDA CARLISLE
DESCRIPTION OF PIECE(S) TOUR BOOK
DESIGN FIRM DESIGN ART, INC.
ART DIRECTOR NORMAN MOORE
DESIGNER NORMAN MOORE
PHOTOGRAPHER VARIOUS

EVENT BELINDA CARLISLE
"RUNAWAY" WORLD TOUR/
BELINDA CARLISLE CONCERT
DESCRIPTION OF PIECE(S) TOUR BOOK
DESIGN FIRM DESIGN ART, INC.
ART DIRECTOR NORMAN MOORE
DESIGNER NORMAN MOORE
PHOTOGRAPHER HERB RITTS
(FRONT COVER), VARIOUS

EVENT 9TH SEATTLE
INTERNATIONAL FILM FESTIVAL
DESCRIPTION OF PIECE(S) POSTER
TYPE DESIGNER NORMAN HATHAWAY
ILLUSTRATOR STEPHEN PERINGER

THE WOMAN'S FACE IS A COMPOSITE OF
FOUR FAMOUS MOVIE STARLETS: LANA
TURNER, HEDDY LAMAR, MARLENE
DIETRICH, AND GENE TIERNEY.

NINTH

Seattle
FILM FESTIVAL

THE
EGYPTIAN
THEATRE
RUNS
THURSDAY
MAY 9
THRU
JUNE 7

EVENT MESQUITE MUSIC FESTIVAL
DESCRIPTION OF PIECE(S) POSTER
DESIGN FIRM SULLIVANPERKINS
ART DIRECTOR RON SULLIVAN
DESIGNER DIANA MCKNIGHT
ILLUSTRATOR DIANA MCKNIGHT

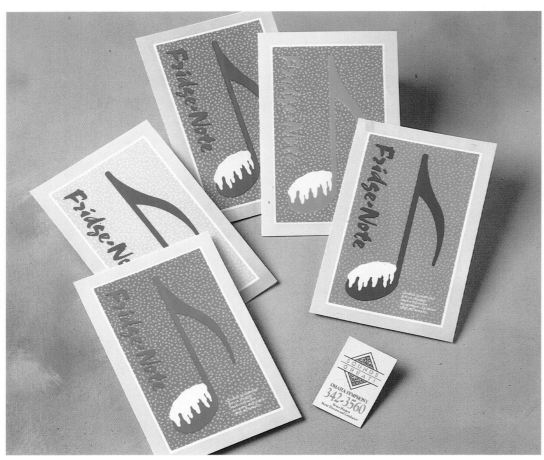

EVENT "FRIDGE NOTES"/OMAHA SYMPHONY
DESCRIPTION OF PIECE(S) POSTER
DESIGN FIRM NEW IDEA DESIGN INC.
DESIGNER RON BOLDT
ILLUSTRATOR RON BOLDT

FIVE FRIDGE NOTES SENT PER SEASON INCLUDE
MAGNET TO STICK THIS CONCERT REMINDER
TO THE FRIDGE.

Event Dance Company: Limón
Description of Piece(s) Poster
Design Firm Russek
Advertising, Inc.
Creative Director James Russek
Designer James Russek
Illustrator Peter Bocour
Photographer Alon

Photo by Alon   Painting by Peter Bocour

LIMÓN
DANCE COMPANY
Carla Maxwell, Artistic Director and Lutz Forster, Associate Artistic Director

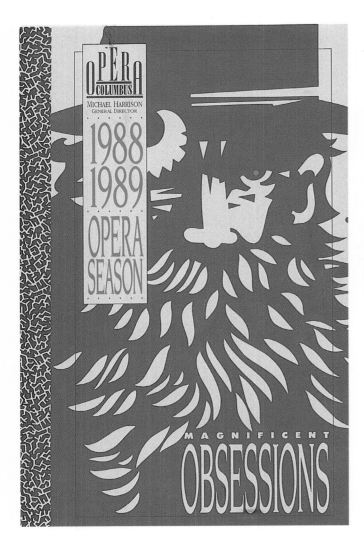

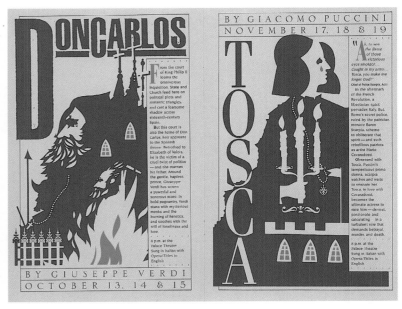

Event Columbus Opera Season
Description of Piece(s) Season brochure
Design Firm Rickabaugh Graphics
Art Director Eric Rickabaugh
Designer Eric Rickabaugh
Illustrator Michael David Brown

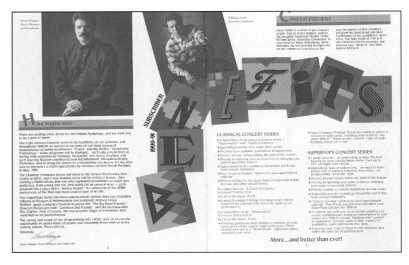

Event Omaha Symphony Season
Description of Piece(s) Brochure
Design Firm New Idea Design Inc.
Designer Kristi McClendon
Illustrator Kristi McClendon

Among usual publicity photos are studio shots of actual concert-goers and their testimonials.

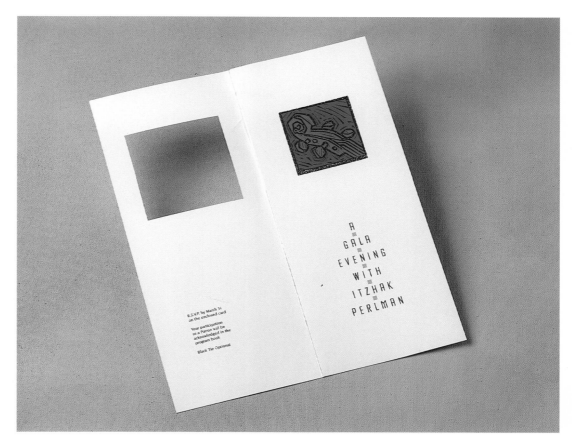

EVENT ITZHAK PERLMAN CONCERT
DESCRIPTION OF PIECE(S) INVITATION TO BENEFIT CONCERT
DESIGN FIRM NEW IDEA DESIGN INC.
DESIGNER RON BOLDT
ILLUSTRATOR RON BOLDT

ILLUSTRATION IS LINEOLEUM CUT, 4 COLORS AND TINT,
VARNISH INSIDE.

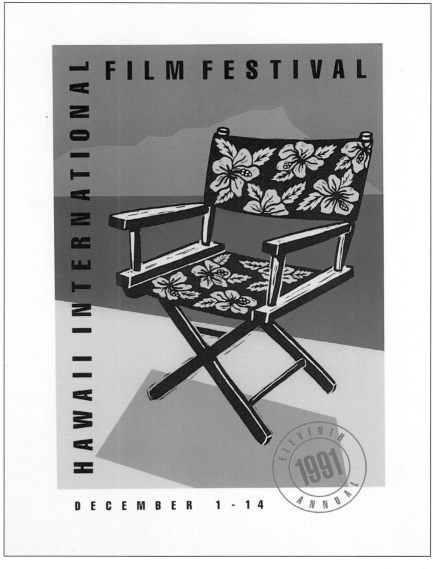

EVENT HAWAII INTERNATIONAL FILM FESTIVAL
DESCRIPTION OF PIECE(S) POSTER
DESIGN FIRM DALE VERMEER DESIGN
ART DIRECTOR DALE VERMEER
DESIGNER DALE VERMEER
ILLUSTRATOR DALE VERMEER

PIECE RECEIVED RECOGNITION IN LOCAL PELE/ADDY
COMPETITION AND WAS FEATURED IN PRINT BOOK.

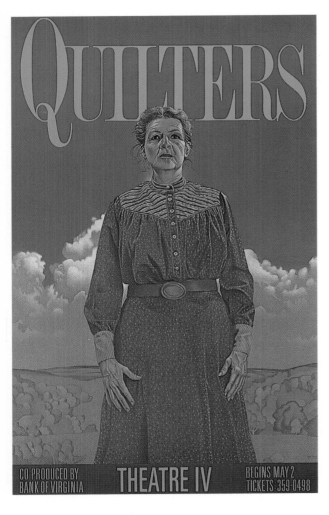

CLOCKWISE FROM TOP LEFT

EVENT "QUILTERS"/THEATRE
DESCRIPTION OF PIECE(S) POSTER
DESIGN FIRM BILL NELSON ILLUSTRATION INC.
ART DIRECTOR BILL NELSON
DESIGNER BILL NELSON
ILLUSTRATOR BILL NELSON

EVENT SEATTLE CAMERATA CONCERT SERIES
DESCRIPTION OF PIECE(S) POSTER
DESIGN FIRM HORNALL ANDERSON DESIGN WORKS
ART DIRECTOR JACK ANDERSON
DESIGNER JACK ANDERSON, DAVID BATES, JULIA LAPINE
ILLUSTRATOR DAVID BATES

EVENT 1993 CINCINNATI OPERA SEASON
DESCRIPTION OF PIECE(S) POSTER
DESIGN FIRM LIBBY PERSZYK KATHMAN
DESIGNER LIZ KATHMAN GRUBOW
ILLUSTRATOR ALAN BROWN, ANGIE FISHER/PHOTONICS GRAPHICS
PHOTOGRAPHER ALAN BROWN/PHOTONICS GRAPHICS

EVENT "THE BEST OF MOBILE"/MOBILE BALLET
DESCRIPTION OF PIECE(S) POSTER
DESIGN FIRM SIMPSON DESIGN INC.
ART DIRECTOR LARRY B. SIMPSON
DESIGNER LARRY B. SIMPSON
PHOTOGRAPHER RICK MOORE

EVENT "SLEEPING BEAUTY"/MOBIL BALLET
DESCRIPTION OF PIECE(S) POSTER
DESIGN FIRM SIMPSON DESIGN INC.
ART DIRECTOR LARRY B. SIMPSON
DESIGNER LARRY B. SIMPSON

EVENT "A SALUTE TO CORPORATE
CHICAGO"/CHICAGO SYMPHONE ORCHESTRA
DESCRIPTION OF PIECE(S) INVITATION AND PROGRAM
DESIGN FIRM LISKA AND ASSOCIATES, INC.
ART DIRECTOR STEVE LISKA
DESIGNER KIM NYBERG
ILLUSTRATOR LINDA BLECK

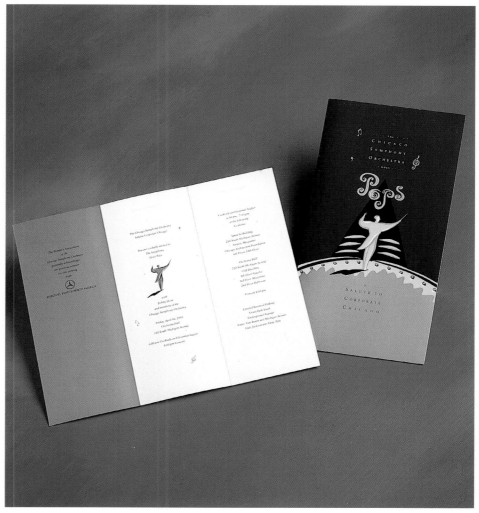

TheaterWorks

Steve Campo, Executive Director

Frankie and Johnny in the Clair de Lune

a comic romance by Terrence McNally

The Hutensky Theater
233 Pearl Street
Downtown Hartford
Fully air-conditioned

Tickets: $15
Students & seniors: $13
Saturdays all tickets $18

For tickets call 527-7838

Recommended for mature adult audiences.

July 16 through
August 15, 1993
Wednesdays through
Saturdays at 8 p.m.
Sundays at 2:30 p.m.

Sponsored by
Bank of Boston Connecticut
and WTIC-TV Fox 61.

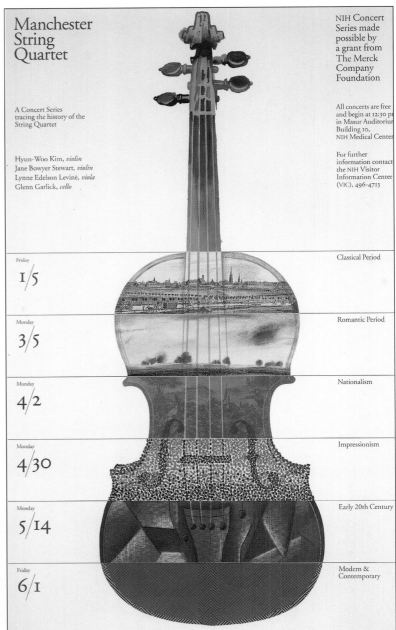

Manchester String Quartet

A Concert Series
tracing the history of the
String Quartet

Hyun-Woo Kim, *violin*
Jane Bowyer Stewart, *violin*
Lynne Edelson Levine, *viola*
Glenn Garlick, *cello*

NIH Concert
Series made
possible by
a grant from
The Merck
Company
Foundation

All concerts are free
and begin at 12:30 pm
in Masur Auditorium
Building 10,
NIH Medical Center

For further
information contact
the NIH Visitor
Information Center
(VIC), 496-4713

Friday 1/5		Classical Period
Monday 3/5		Romantic Period
Monday 4/2		Nationalism
Monday 4/30		Impressionism
Monday 5/14		Early 20th Century
Friday 6/1		Modern & Contemporary

The Headless Horseman of Sleepy Hollow

World Premiere
of Jon Deak's composition
based on Washington Irving's
American Classic.
Mstislav Rostropovich
conducting the
National Symphony Orchestra
and the Manchester String Quartet

Commissioned by the
Merck Company Foundation in 1991
in celebration of the centennial
of Merck & Co., Inc.

Manchester String Quartet:
Hyun-Woo Kim, violin
Jane Bowyer Stewart, violin
Nancy Thomas Bittner, viola
Glenn Garlick, cello

Kennedy Center Concert Hall

January 30 and February 1, 1992
8:30 pm

February 4, 1992
7:00 pm

CLOCKWISE FROM TOP LEFT

Event Frankie and Johnny in the Clair de Lune
Description of Piece(s) Poster
Design Firm Peter Good Graphic Design
Art Director Peter Good
Designer Peter Good
Illustrator Peter Good

Event Manchester String Quartet
Description of Piece(s) Poster
Design Firm Peter Good Graphic Design
Art Director Peter Good
Designer Peter Good
Illustrator Peter Good

Event Headless Horseman
Description of Piece(s) Poster
Design Firm Peter Good Graphic Design
Art Director Peter Good
Designer Peter Good
Illustrator Peter Good

CREATIVE DIRECTOR PETER GOOD
DESIGNER PETER GOOD
ILLUSTRATOR PETER GOOD
PHOTOGRAPHER JIM COON

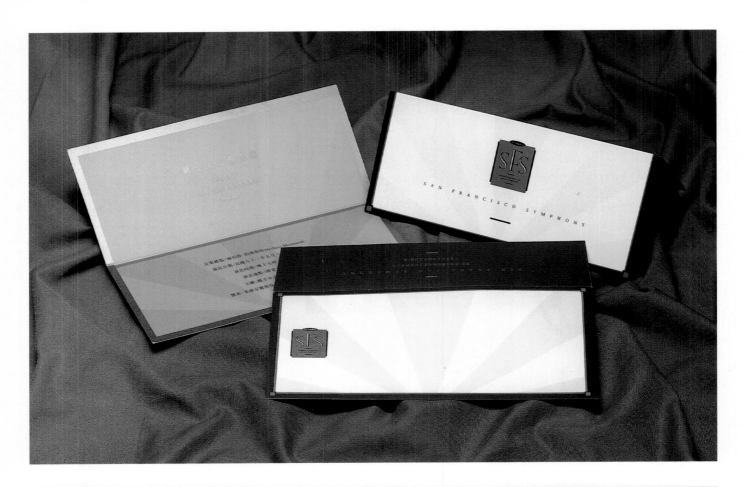

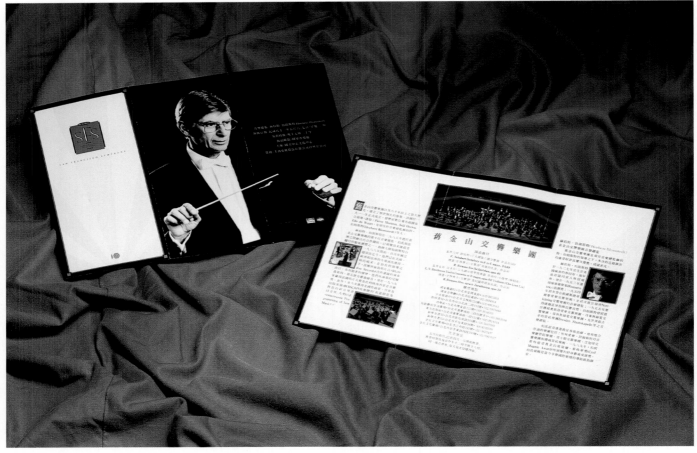

EVENT SAN FRANCISCO SYMPHONY
DESIGN FIRM LESLIE CHAN DESIGN CO., LTD.
ART DIRECTOR LESLIE CHAN WING KEI
DESIGNER LESLIE CHAN WING KEI,
  TONG SONG WEI, TOTO TSENG

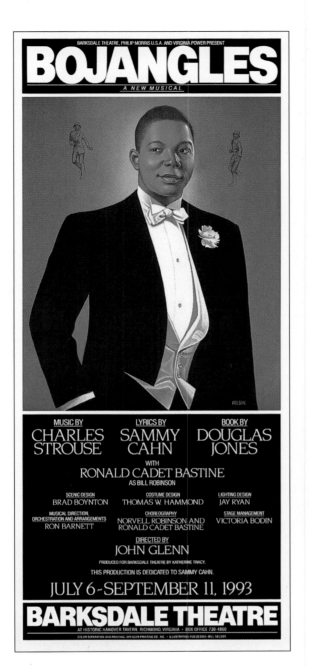

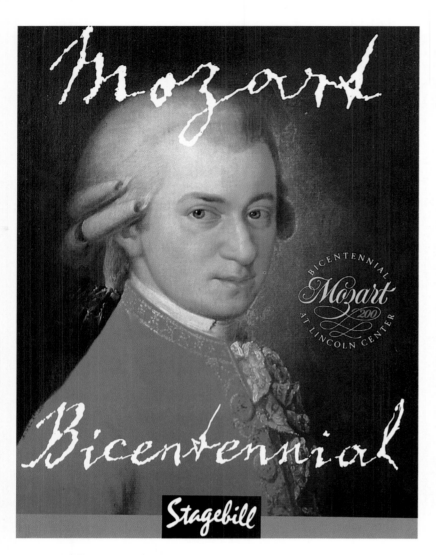

EVENT MOZART BICENTENNIAL
DESCRIPTION OF PIECE(S) SOUVENIR BOOK
DESIGN FIRM STAGEBILL
ART DIRECTOR ALEX STARK
DESIGNER ALEX STARK
ILLUSTRATOR BARBARA KRAFFT

EVENT A SHOW OF ACCOMPLISHMENT
DESCRIPTION OF PIECE(S) ANNOUCEMENT,
TICKET STUFFER, PROGRAM
DESIGN FIRM RICKABAUGH GRAPHICS
ART DIRECTOR ERIC RICKABAUGH
DESIGNER MARK KRUMEL

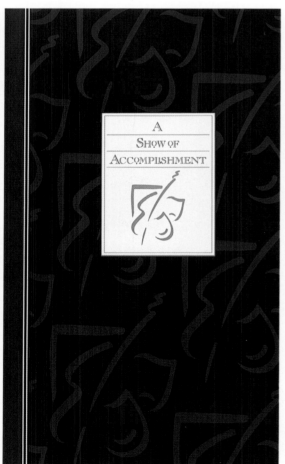

PROFILE

The mastery of Pinchas Zukerman defines the true meaning of artist. Violinist, violist, conductor, teacher, chamber musician, and champion of young artists, Mr. Zukerman is recognized throughout the world as an extraordinary musician. In 1983 President Reagan presented him with a Medal of Arts honoring him as a leader in the musical world. Though critically acclaimed for his music genius and technical prowess, perhaps the most compelling aspect of his presence is an exceptional combination of integrity and zeal.

He was born in Tel Aviv in 1948 and began his musical training with his father. At age eight, he began studying at the Israel Conservatory and the Academy of Music in Tel Aviv. With the guidance of Isaac Stern and Pablo Casals, the support of the American-Israel Cultural Foundation and scholarships from Juilliard and the Helena Rubinstein Foundation, he came to America in 1962 to study with Ivan Galamian at the Juilliard School. In 1967, Mr. Zukerman won First Prize in the Twenty-Fifth Leventritt International Competition, setting the stage for his solo career.

Among his numerous achievements, Mr. Zukerman's prolific discography numbers more than seventy-five releases and is widely representative of the violin and viola repertoire. His internationally acclaimed recordings for Angel, CBS Masterworks, Deutsche Grammophon, London Records, Philips Classics, and RCA have garnered nineteen Grammy nominations and two awards:

"Best Chamber Music Performance" in 1980 and "Best Classical Performance—Instrumental Soloist with Orchestra" in 1981. Recent recordings include Schoenberg's "Pierrot Lunaire" and the Berg Violin Concerto.

Pinchas Zukerman's conducting career began in 1970 with the English Chamber Orchestra, and he has since conducted many of the world's leading orchestras including the New York Philharmonic, the Boston Symphony, the Los Angeles Philharmonic, the Berlin Philharmonic, the London Symphony Orchestra, and the Israel Philharmonic. He served as Music Director of the South Bank Festival for three years and the St. Paul Chamber Orchestra for seven years. In the summer of 1990, Mr. Zukerman began a three-year appointment as Principal Guest Conductor of the Dallas Symphony Orchestra's new International Music Festival. The Festival received critical acclaim for the high caliber of concerts throughout the three-week celebration.

Featured in numerous television specials, Pinchas Zukerman was recently a guest artist in a "Live from Lincoln Center" concert with the Chamber Music Society. A PBS special titled "Mozart by the Masters" with the Chicago Symphony and colleagues Itzhak Perlman and Victor Borge aired nationally last year. Zukerman has participated in several collaborations with the English director Christopher Nupen including the "Here to Make Music" series, a Brahms series, and a Schubert series.

PINCHAS ZUKERMAN

9

EVENT DANCING AT LUGHNASA/
PITTSBURGH PUBLIC THEATER
DESCRIPTION OF PIECE(S) POSTER
DESIGN FIRM LYNNE CANNOY DESIGN
ART DIRECTOR LYNNE CANNOY
DESIGNER LYNNE CANNOY
ILLUSTRATOR LYNNE CANNOY

EVENT ITZHAK PERLMAN CONCERT
DESCRIPTION OF PIECE(S) INVITATION TO GALA
DESIGN FIRM NEW IDEA DESIGN INC.
DESIGNER KRISTI MCCLENDON
ILLUSTRATOR RON BOLDT

"236" IS THE NUMBER OF INDIVIDUAL
STRINGS ON INSTRUMENTS IN THE
ORCHESTRA, INCLUDING PERLMAN.

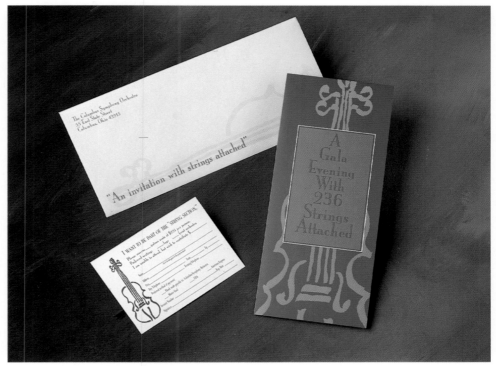

THE SANTA FE OPERA

John Crosby, General Director
Post Office Box 2408
Santa Fe, New Mexico 87504-2408
Box Office: (505)982-3855

Address Correction Requested

THIRTY-FIFTH SEASON
JUNE 28–AUGUST 24, 1991

THE
MUSIC.
THE MAGIC.
THE MOON & STARS.
THE SANTA FE OPERA.

ORDERING INFORMATION

GALA OPENING Our 35th Season opens June 28th with a gala performance of LA TRAVIATA, preceded by our traditional reception on the theater terraces for the entire audience. The evening concludes with waltzing under the stars to music performed by our Orchestra. For information regarding additional Gala Events such as the Opera Ball, Pre-Opera Dinners and the Southwest Barbecue, please contact the Special Events Office, (505-982-3851).

TELEPHONE ORDERS Call (505) 982-3855 to use your American Express, MasterCard or VISA from 10:00 AM to 4:00 PM, Monday through Friday. Also open Saturdays beginning May 25. Please have your brochure and credit card ready when calling. There is a $2.00 per ticket handling charge on all telephone orders.

MAIL ORDERS Since many sections sell out early, please list preferred and alternate choices on the order form. A $2.00 per ticket handling charge is added to each mail order.

BOX OFFICE LOCATION AND HOURS (*In-person sales only*):

DOWNTOWN SANTA FE Beginning April 1, Galisteo News & Ticket Center at Galisteo and Water Streets, Monday through Friday, 10:00 AM-1:00 PM and 2:00 PM-4:00 PM. Also open Saturdays beginning May 25.

OPERA THEATER BOX OFFICE Beginning May 25, Monday through Saturday, 10:00 AM-4:00 PM and through the first intermission on performance evenings.

LIBRETTI AND SYNOPSES Enhance your enjoyment of the opera with these explanatory guides. Synopses offer plot summaries of all 1991 productions, while a Libretto gives the full script and translation when applicable. (See Order Form.)

PRE-OPERA BUFFETS Start your evening on the Opera grounds with a buffet supper hosted by The Guilds of The Santa Fe Opera. 6:30 PM; $30.00 per person (includes $15.00 contribution). See Calendar and Order Form for dates.

STANDING ROOM $5.00 for all performances except the Gala Opening (Friday, June 28 - $10.00). On sale at 8:00 PM at the Theater Box Office on performance evenings.

HANDICAPPED Opera seating is accessible to handicapped patrons. Please contact the Box Office. Tickets for wheelchair accommodations are $10.00 for all performances except the Gala Opening (Friday, June 28 - $20.00).

TRANSPORTATION The Santa Fe Opera is located 7 miles north of Santa Fe on Highway 84-285. Ample parking is available. To avoid traffic congestion, patrons should arrive at the theater parking lot before 8:30 PM. There are a number of services that provide transportation to and from the Opera. For further information, contact the Box Office or the Santa Fe Chamber of Commerce, P.O. Box 1928, Santa Fe, NM 87504-1928, (505) 983-7317.

GIFT CERTIFICATE The perfect gift for any occasion. Delight your favorite music lover with a gift certificate of $25, $50 or $100. For information, contact the Box Office.

1991 PERFORMANCE SCHEDULE

JUNE

MON	TUE	WED	THU	FRI	SAT
24	25	26	27	28 LA TRAVIATA	29 LE NOZZE DI FIGARO
				Gala Opening Weekend	

JULY

MON	TUE	WED	THU	FRI	SAT
1	2	3 LE NOZZE DI FIGARO	4 LA TRAVIATA	5 LE NOZZE DI FIGARO	6 LA TRAVIATA
8	9	10 LA TRAVIATA	11	12 LE NOZZE DI FIGARO	13 LA FANCIULLA DEL WEST*
15	16	17 LA FANCIULLA DEL WEST	18	19 LA TRAVIATA	20 DIE SCHWEIGSAME FRAU
22	23	24 DIE SCHWEIGSAME FRAU	25	26 LA FANCIULLA DEL WEST	27 OEDIPUS*
29 LE NOZZE DI FIGARO	30 LA TRAVIATA	31 OEDIPUS*			

AUGUST

MON	TUE	WED	THU	FRI	SAT
			1 LE NOZZE DI FIGARO	2 DIE SCHWEIGSAME FRAU	3 LA FANCIULLA DEL WEST
5 LA TRAVIATA	6 LE NOZZE DI FIGARO	7 LA FANCIULLA DEL WEST	8 DIE SCHWEIGSAME FRAU	9 OEDIPUS	10 LE NOZZE DI FIGARO
12 APPRENTICE ARTISTS' CONCERT I	13 LA TRAVIATA*	14 LE NOZZE DI FIGARO	15 DIE SCHWEIGSAME FRAU	16 LA FANCIULLA DEL WEST	17 OEDIPUS
19 APPRENTICE ARTISTS' CONCERT II	20 LA TRAVIATA	21 DIE SCHWEIGSAME FRAU	22 LA FANCIULLA DEL WEST	23 LE NOZZE DI FIGARO*	24 LA TRAVIATA

†$5.00 for general admission.
*Pre-Opera Buffet on the opera grounds begins at 6:30 PM.
Repertory, casts and dates subject to change.

APPRENTICE ARTISTS' CONCERTS August 12th and 19th. Each Monday evening concert features talent from the most coveted training program in America. At $5.00 for general admission you can't afford to miss either one!

BACKSTAGE TOURS Discover the excitement behind the scenes beginning July 1 through August 24 (Monday through Saturday at 2:00 PM). The charge for the one-hour tour is $5.00 (free for children 7 to 15).

DONATED TICKETS When unable to attend a performance, your tickets may be donated to the Box Office by 8:45 PM on the evening of the performance. The ticket value is tax-deductible and a receipt will be issued.

THE
SANTA FE
OPERA
1991 SEASON

JUNE 28–AUGUST 24

Giuseppe Verdi
LA TRAVIATA

Wolfgang Amadeus Mozart
LE NOZZE DI FIGARO

Giacomo Puccini
LA FANCIULLA DEL WEST

Richard Strauss
DIE SCHWEIGSAME FRAU

Wolfgang Rihm
OEDIPUS
(American Premiere)

Come celebrate our 35th Season. Filled with the magic of music and moonlight – each evening becomes an unforgettable experience. Blending seasoned classics, overlooked treasures and significant premieres, we proudly offer you an exciting repertory in an exquisite southwestern setting. Celebrate the splendor of opera at it's best. Reserve your tickets now!

Giuseppe Verdi's "La Traviata" (1989)

Richard Strauss' "Die Schweigsame Frau" (1987)

Richard Strauss' "Ariadne auf Naxos" (1990)

FACING PAGES

EVENT SANTA FE OPERA
DESCRIPTION OF PIECE(S) TICKET BROCHURE
DESIGN FIRM VAUGHN WEDEEN CREATIVE
ART DIRECTOR RICK VAUGHN
DESIGNER RICK VAUGHN
ILLUSTRATOR BILL GERHOLD, HEIDI SMITH

LE NOZZE DI FIGARO

WOLFGANG AMADEUS MOZART

NEW PRODUCTION
Performances on
June 29, July 3, 5, 12, 29,
August 1, 6, 10, 14, 25
Sung in Italian
First performed at Vienna in 1786

CONDUCTOR
Edo de Waart
(June 29, July 3, 5, 12, 29, August 1, 6)
George Manahan
(August 10, 14, 25)

DIRECTOR
John Cox

SCENIC & COSTUME DESIGN
Robert Perdziola

LIGHTING DESIGN
Craig Miller

CAST
Figaro   Bryn Terfel
Susanna   Heidi Grant
Countess Almaviva   Sheri Greenawald
Count Almaviva   Michael Devlin
Cherubino   Susan Graham
Marcellina   Joyce Castle
Don Basilio   John Fryatt
Dr. Bartolo   François Loup
Don Curzio   Darren Keith Woods
Antonio   John Kuether

Once a revolutionary social commentary, Beaumarchais' play about a Count, Countess and their plotting servants emerges from Mozart's hands as an enchanting insight into the workings of the human heart.

Performances on
July 20, 24,
August 2, 8, 15, 21
Sung in English
First performed at Dresden in 1935

CONDUCTOR
John Crosby

PRODUCTION
Göran Järvefelt

DIRECTOR
Ken Cazan

SCENIC & COSTUME DESIGN
Carl Friedrich Oberle

LIGHTING DESIGN
Kim Davis

CAST
Aminta   Erie Mills
Sir John Morosus   Eric Halfvarson
The Barber   David Malis
Henry Morosus   Mark Thomsen
The Housekeeper   Joyce Castle
Isotta   Sally Wolf
Carlotta   Judith Christin
Vanuzzi   François Loup
Morbio   Gimi Beni
Farfallo   James Ramlet

Comic disguises and chicanery lead to confusion in Strauss' colorful account of a stubborn recluse who decides to defy his nephew by marrying, but only if he can find "a silent woman."

Die Schweigsame Frau
RICHARD STRAUSS

NEW PRODUCTION
(American Premiere)
Performances on
July 27, 31,
August 9, 17
Sung in English
First performed at Berlin in 1987

CONDUCTOR
George Manahan

DIRECTOR
Francesca Zambello

SCENIC & COSTUME DESIGN
Bruno Schwengl

LIGHTING DESIGN
Craig Miller

CAST
Oedipus   Rodney Gilfry
Jocasta   Emily Golden
Kreon   David Rampy
Tiresias   William Dooley
Bote   Peter Van Derick
Hirte   Patryk Wroblewski

Rihm's score brings this chilling myth to life as the innocent Oedipus unknowingly destroys his father and sets in motion the tragic chain of events culminating in his downfall.

WOLFGANG RIHM
OEDIPUS

Performances on
June 28, July 4, 6, 10, 19, 30,
August 5, 13, 20, 24
Sung in Italian
First performed at Venice in 1853

CONDUCTOR
John Crosby
(June 28, July 4, 6, 10)
John Fiore
(July 19, 30, August 5, 13, 20, 24)

PRODUCTION
John Copley

DIRECTOR
Laurie Feldman

SCENIC DESIGN
Robert Perdziola

COSTUME DESIGN
Michael Stennett

LIGHTING DESIGN
Craig Miller

CHOREOGRAPHER
Rodney Griffin

CAST
Violetta Valery   Janice Hall
Alfredo Germont   Fernando de la Mora
Giorgio Germont   William Stone
Marquis d'Obigny   Peter Van Derick
Dr. Grenvil   James Ramlet

The elegant world of the Parisian demimonde is the backdrop to Verdi's passionate story of honor and loyalty, as a beautiful courtesan sacrifices her own happiness for true love.

La Traviata
GIUSEPPE VERDI

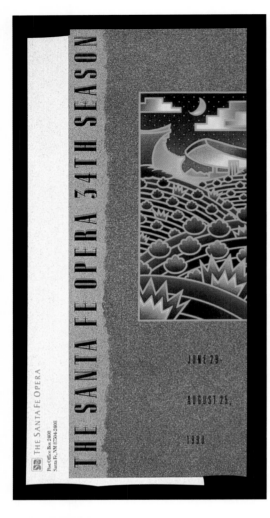

THE SANTA FE OPERA 34TH SEASON

JUNE 29–
AUGUST 25,
1990

THE SANTA FE OPERA
Post Office Box 2408
Santa Fe, NM 87504-2408

The Santa Fe Opera Theater

THE SANTA FE OPERA   34TH SEASON

LA BOHÈME
Giacomo Puccini

COSÌ FAN TUTTE
Wolfgang Amadeus Mozart

ORFEO ED EURIDICE
Christoph Willibald Gluck

ARIADNE AUF NAXOS
Richard Strauss

JUDITH
Siegfried Matthus
(American Premiere)

Excitement blossoms during summer amid the beautiful Sangre de Cristo mountains of Northern New Mexico—the splendor of opera at its best. Blending seasoned classics, neglected masterpieces and significant premieres, The Santa Fe Opera is internationally recognized as an artistic treasure.

News of the Day
(1981)

Reserve your tickets now and join in the celebration of operatic rapture in an exquisite outdoor setting.

Design & Illustration: Vaughn Wedeen Creative, Inc.
Photography: Murrae Haynes, David Stein, Michael Rouetschal, Hans Fahrmeyer

ORFEO ED EURIDICE

GLUCK

Gluck's score brings the classic tale of Orfeo's epic journey to life, as his quest for Euridice takes him to the underworld and back.

ORFEO ED EURIDICE
Christoph Willibald Gluck
July 14, 18, 27
August 4, 8, 17, 23
Sung in Italian

Conductor
Lawrence Foster

Director
Lamont Johnson

Choreographer
Kimi Okada

Scenic and Costume Design
Steven Rubin

Shadow Master
Larry Reed

Lighting Design
Craig Miller

Cast
Orfeo
Marilyn Horne
Euridice
Benita Valente
Amor
Tracy Dahl

This production is made possible in part by a generous grant from the Eleanor Naylor Dana Charitable Trust.

SUBSCRIBE NOW
AND ENJOY THESE
SPECIAL PRIVILEGES!

As a Subscriber, you are a very special part of The Santa Fe Opera.

L'Orione
(1983)

Increased Selection. Whether it be a full- or mini-series, there's sure to be a subscription that meets your busy summer schedule. Create your own mini-series with a minimum of three dates from any full-series.

Free Synopses. Stories of all the productions to read in advance are mailed with your tickets.

Renewal Benefits. Subscribers have first options on the same seating year after year. You will also receive top priority should you decide to change your seating or series next season. If you would like further information and assistance or prefer to order by telephone, call the Box Office at (505) 982-3855.

Special Events. You will be invited to many exciting events throughout the summer including pre-opera festivities, discussions and forums.

Ticket Insurance. Your seat is on file and guaranteed. If your ticket is lost, we will duplicate it free of charge.

Daphne
(1981)

EVENT SANTA FE OPERA
DESCRIPTION OF PIECE(S) TICKET BROCHURE
DESIGN FIRM VAUGHN WEDEEN CREATIVE
ART DIRECTOR RICK VAUGHN
DESIGNER RICK VAUGHN
ILLUSTRATOR KEVIN TOLMAN, RICK VAUGHN

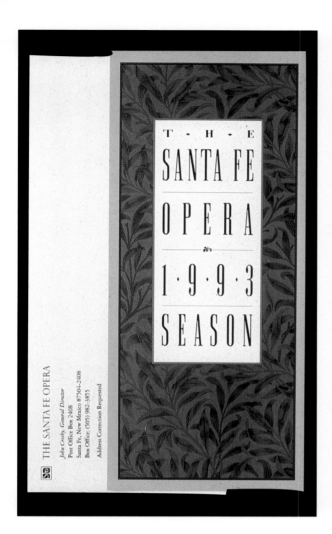

THE SANTA FE OPERA

John Crosby, General Director
Post Office Box 2408
Santa Fe, New Mexico 87504-2408
Box Office: (505) 982-3855
Address Correction Requested

T·H·E

SANTA FE OPERA

1·9·9·3

SEASON

The Santa Fe Opera celebrates 37 seasons of music under the stars. Blending seasoned classics, overlooked treasures and significant premieres, this unique repertory offers something for everyone. Let the enchantment begin.

1 9 9 3 SEASON
July 2 - August 28

Giacomo Puccini
LA BOHÈME

Wolfgang Amadeus Mozart
THE MAGIC FLUTE

George Frederick Handel
XERXES

Richard Strauss
CAPRICCIO

Kurt Weill
THE PROTAGONIST
and
THE TSAR HAS HIS PHOTOGRAPH TAKEN

EVENT SANTA FE OPERA
DESCRIPTION OF PIECE(S) TICKET BROCHURE
DESIGN FIRM VAUGHN WEDEEN CREATIVE
ART DIRECTOR RICK VAUGHN
DESIGNER LISA GRAFF

THIS SUMMER, DISCOVER AN INTERNATIONAL ART TREASURE

Santa Fe has been a mecca for adventurers in the arts for centuries, melding many distinctive cultures in an unparalleled setting of natural beauty. Treat yourself to a creative vacation at one of the most beautiful destinations in the world.

For over three decades, The Santa Fe Opera has been an international leader in opera production, a spectac-

ular medium embracing music, design, dance and drama. We invite you to expe-rience the emotional power that awaits you at our 37th Season Celebration.

Enjoy an exquisite sunset as prelude to your evening of enchantment. As music fills the night air, you are transported to another time and place. Reserve your seats now and explore a world waiting to be discovered.

GALA OPENING NIGHT

Make plans now to usher in the 1993 season in style by attending the Opening Night performance of La Bohème on Friday, July 2. Preceded by a sparkling champagne recep-tion on the theater terrace (free for the entire audience), your evening of enchantment concludes with onstage waltzing under the stars to music performed by The Santa Fe Opera Orchestra.

GALA OPENING WEEKEND CELEBRATION

Join us for one of the premier social events of the Southwest as a Benefactor or Patron at the 1993 Gala Opening Weekend Celebration. Beginning Thursday, July 1, with the Opera Ball, the celebration continues with preferred seating at the Opening Night performance, and the opening night of our new production of The Magic Flute on July 3 (for Benefactors). Festivities throughout the weekend include special pre-opera dinners in private homes, the Benefactor Dinner on the Opera Grounds with performances by our Apprentice Artists, and a Southwestern Independence Day Barbecue. Proceeds from the Gala benefit our acclaimed Apprentice Programs for Singers and Technicians. For additional information regarding the Gala Celebration, please contact the Special Events Office (505) 982-3851. Reservations for this exclusive weekend of events are limited.

EVENT "MARIN BALLET"
DESCRIPTION OF PIECE(S) POSTER
DESIGN FIRM SACKETT DESIGN ASSOCIATES
ART DIRECTOR MARK SACKETT
DESIGNER MARK SACKETT, WAYNE SAKAMOTO
ILLUSTRATOR CHRIS YARYAN

EVENT SANTA FE OPERA
DESCRIPTION OF PIECE(S) TICKET BROCHURE
DESIGN FIRM VAUGHN WEDEEN CREATIVE
ART DIRECTOR RICK VAUGHN
DESIGNER RICK VAUGHN
ILLUSTRATOR JOZEF BAKER (COVER),
GARY KELLEY (INSIDE)

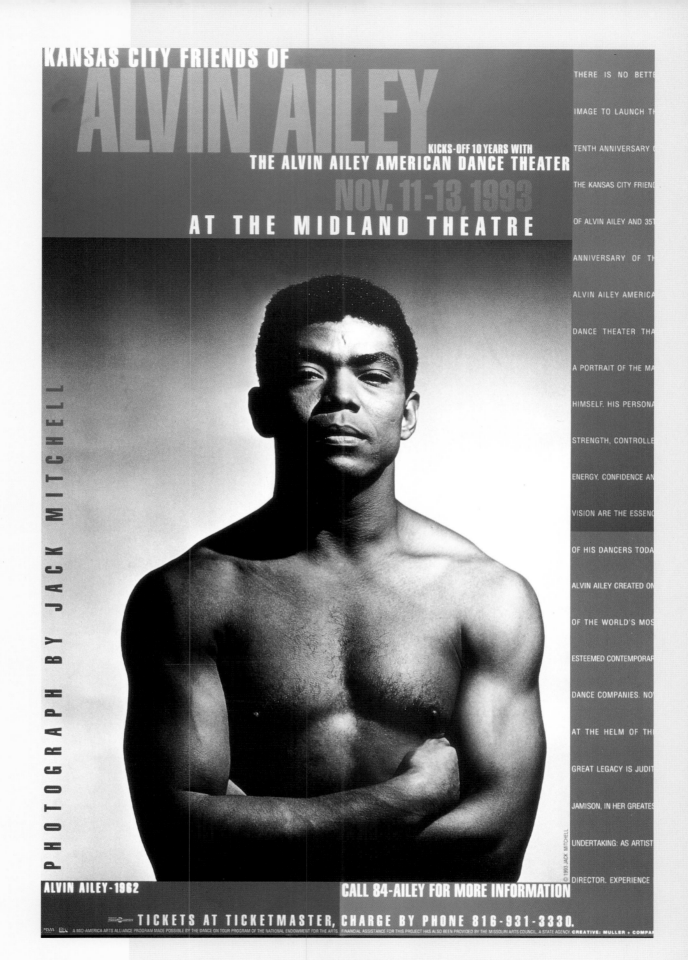

EVENT ALVIN AILEY
DESCRIPTION OF PIECE(S) POSTER
DESIGN FIRM MULLER + COMPANY
ART DIRECTOR JOHN MULLER
DESIGNER MIKE MILLER
PHOTOGRAPHER JACK MITCHELL

57

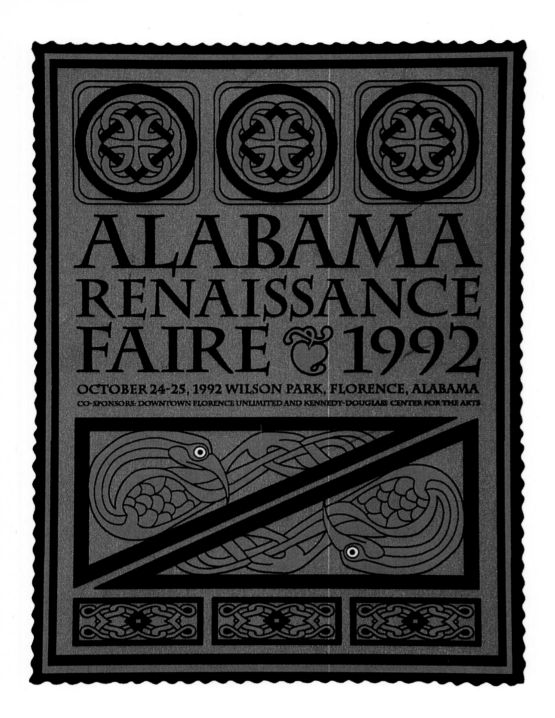

EVENT ALABAMA RENAISSANCE FAIR
DESCRIPTION OF PIECE(S) POSTER
DESIGN FIRM SIMPSON DESIGN INC.
ART DIRECTOR LARRY B. SIMPSON
DESIGNER LARRY B. SIMPSON

EVENT CINCINNATI BALLET
DESCRIPTION OF PIECE(S) POSTER
DESIGN FIRM CATT LYON DESIGN INC.
ART DIRECTOR CHARLENE CATT LYON
DESIGNER CHARLENE CATT LYON
PHOTOGRAPHER ALAN BROWN/PHOTO DESIGN

CINCINNATI *Pops* ORCHESTRA
ERICH KUNZEL • CONDUCTOR

CINCINNATI *Symphony* ORCHESTRA
JESÚS LÓPEZ-COBOS • MUSIC DIRECTOR

CSO 100

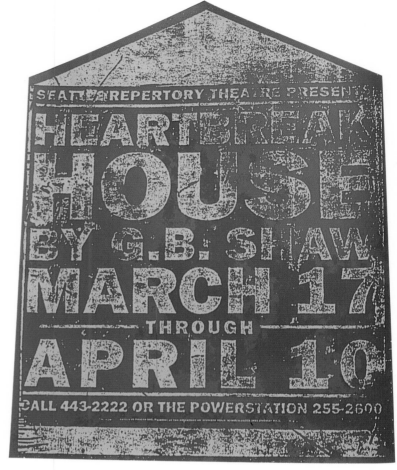

CLOCKWISE FROM TOP LEFT

Event CINCINNATI SYMPHONY ORCHESTRA
Description of Piece(s) LOGOS
Design Firm CATT LYON DESIGN INC.
Art Director CHARLENE CATT LYON
Designer CHARLENE CATT LYON

Event "HEARTBREAK HOUSE"/THEATRE
Description of Piece(s) POSTER (SCREENPRINTED)
Design Firm MODERN DOG
Art Director VITTORIO COSTARELLA,
DOUGLAS HUGHES
Designer VITTORIO COSTARELLA

Event "THE LISBON TRAVIATA"/THEATRE
Description of Piece(s) POSTER
Design Firm MODERN DOG
Art Director ROBYNNE RAYE
Designer ROBYNNE RAYE

EVENT THE ROYAL CONCERTGEBOW ORCHESTRA
DESCRIPTION OF PIECE(S) BROCHURE, CARD
DESIGN FIRM LESLIE CHAN DESIGN CO., LTD.
ART DIRECTOR LESLIE CHAN WING KEI
DESIGNER LESLIE CHANG WING KEI,
   TONG SONG WEI

furnish your mind

EVENT NEOCON
DESCRIPTION OF PIECE(S) BROCHURE, STATIONERY, POSTCARDS,
     DIRECT MAIL, POSTER
DESIGN FIRM SEGURA INC.
ART DIRECTOR CARLOS SEGURA
DESIGNER CARLOS SEGURA
PHOTOGRAPHER GEOF KERN

NEOCON/92
THE WORLD EXPOSITION ON WORKPLACE PLANNING AND DESIGN

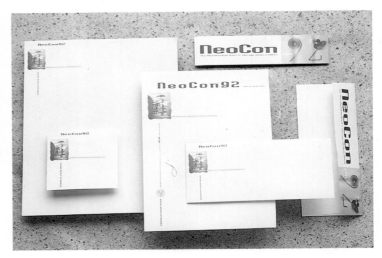

62

EVENT MELBOURNE INTERNATIONAL ARTS FESTIVAL
DESCRIPTION OF PIECE(S) BANNER, POSTER,
LEAFLET, T-SHIRT, PROGRAM
DESIGN FIRM CATO DESIGN INC.
DESIGNER KEN CATO

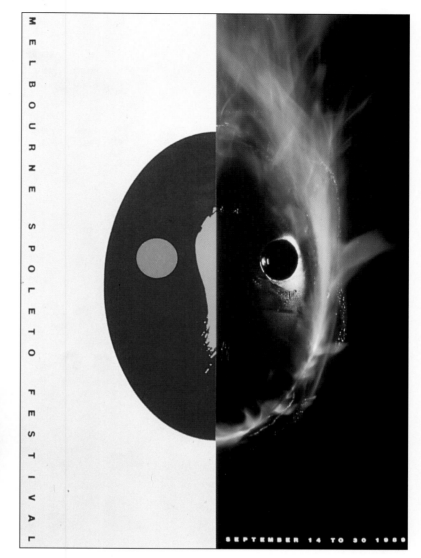

EVENT SCIENCEWORKS MUSEUM
DESCRIPTION OF PIECE(S) SIGNAGE, BAG, T-SHIRT
DESIGN FIRM CATO DESIGN INC.
DESIGNER KEN CATO

EVENT INTERMATION TRADE SHOW EXHIBIT
DESCRIPTION OF PIECE(S) STATIONERY, BROCHURE, EXHIBIT
DESIGN FIRM HORNALL ANDERSON DESIGN WORKS
ART DIRECTOR JACK ANDERSON
DESIGNER JACK ANDERSON, LEO RAYMUNDO,
JULIA LAPINE, JILL BUSTAMANTE
ILLUSTRATOR LEO RAYMUNDO
COPYWRITER BILL ROZIER

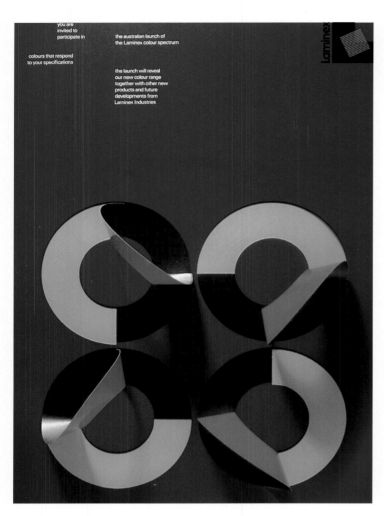

EVENT LAMINEX INDUSTRIES EXHIBITION
DESCRIPTION OF PIECE(S) 3-D SCULPTURES
DESIGN FIRM CATO DESIGN INC.
DESIGNER KEN CATO

EVENT DINOSAUR MUSEUM SHOW
DESCRIPTION OF PIECE(S) BANNERS,
BUS SHELTERS, T-SHIRTS
DESIGN FIRM MIKE QUON DESIGN OFFICE
ART DIRECTOR GRO FRUVOU
DESIGNER MIKE QUON
ILLUSTRATOR MIKE QUON

EVENT CELEBRATION OF FINE ARTS PROGRAM/
SOUTHWEST TEXAS STATE UNIVERSITY
DESCRIPTION OF PIECE(S) BROCHURE, POSTERS, PINS
DESIGN FIRM THE BRADFORD LAWTON DESIGN GROUP
ART DIRECTOR BRADFORD LAWTON, WILLIAM MEEK
DESIGNER BRADFORD LAWTON, JODY LANEY
ILLUSTRATOR BRADFORD LAWTON, JODY LANEY

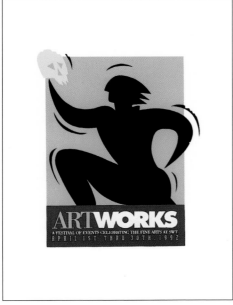

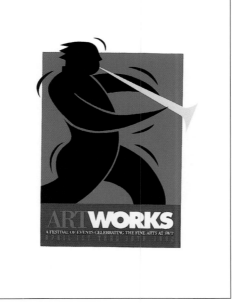

Event La Quinta Arts Festival
Description of Piece(s) Billboard,
PLAYBILL, POSTCARD
Design Firm Mark Palmer Design
Art Director Mark Palmer
Designer Mark Palmer, Pat Kellog
Illustrator Pat Kellog
Symbol Concepts Andrew Nelson

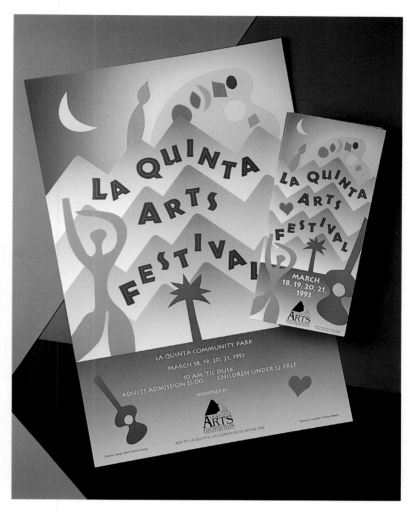

Event Fine Crafts, Wine and All That Jazz
Description of Piece(s) Poster board,
PLAYBILL, POSTCARD
Design Firm Mark Palmer Design
Art Director Mark Palmer
Designer Mark Palmer, Pat Kellogg
Illustrator Mark Palmer, Curtis Palmer
Symbol Concept Andrew Nelson

69

There's no time like the present to prepare for Christmas future.

This year, the truly gifted will see the colors of Christmas in July.

CLOCKWISE FROM TOP LEFT

EVENT CENTRAL PHILADELPHIA FESTIVAL OF THE ARTS
DESCRIPTION OF PIECE(S) POSTER
DESIGN FIRM SOMMESE DESIGN
ART DIRECTOR LANNY SOMMESE
DESIGNER LANNY SOMMESE
ILLUSTRATOR LANNY SOMMESE

ANNUAL EVENT OF THE VISUAL AND PERFORMING ARTS

EVENT ANNUAL SUMMER EVENT FOR THE VISUAL & PERFORMING ARTS
DESCRIPTION OF PIECE(S) POSTER
DESIGN FIRM SOMMESE DESIGN
ART DIRECTOR LANNY SOMMESE
DESIGNER KRISTIN SOMMESE
ILLUSTRATOR LANNY SOMMESE

25TH ANNIVERSARY OF THE EVENT

EVENT CHRISTMAS IN JULY SHOW
DESCRIPTION OF PIECE(S) POSTCARDS
DESIGN FIRM SEGURA INC.
ART DIRECTOR CARLOS SEGURA
DESIGNER CARLOS SEGURA

Event Annual Summer Event for the Visual and Performing Arts
Description of Piece(s) Poster
Design Firm Sommese Design
Art Director Lanny Sommese
Designer Lanny Sommese
Illustrator Lanny Sommese

Event Promotional Brochure Series
Description of Piece(s) Information, membership, floor plan brochures
Design Firm Guggenheim Museum
Art Director Cara Galowitz
Designer Cara Galowitz

Brochures are displayed in a rack in specific order and build image of the Guggenheim.

Event Point of Contact Art Exhibition
Description of Piece(s) Catalog
Design Firm Northern Illinois University, Office of Publications
Art Director Tadson O. Bussey
Designer Tadson O. Bussey
Editor Mary Wiegele, Kirstin Ruby
Photographer Dan Grych

This catalog is hand-bound with Japanese rice paper and bamboo and hand-stamped with initial-cap.

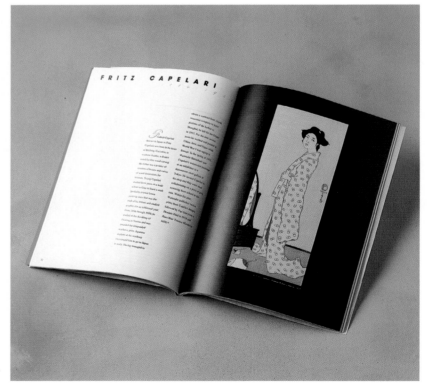

EVENT AQUARIUM SHOW
DESCRIPTION OF PIECE(S) POSTER (4-COLOR)
DESIGN FIRM LINDA S. SHERMAN DESIGN, INC.
ART DIRECTOR LINDA S. SHERMAN
DESIGNER LINDA SHERMAN, EILEEN O'TOUSA
ILLUSTRATOR LINDA SHERMAN

EVENT AQUARIUM FOR WILDLIFE CONSERVATION
DESCRIPTION OF PIECE(S) SUBWAY POSTER
CREATIVE DIRECTOR RODNEY UNDERWOOD
ART DIRECTOR JEFF VOGT, DAVID TESSLER

EVENT BRONX ZOO/WILDLIFE CONSERVATION PARK
DESCRIPTION OF PIECE(S) SUBWAY POSTER
CREATIVE DIRECTOR RODNEY UNDERWOOD
ART DIRECTOR JEFF VOGT, DAVID TESSLER

THIS NOT-FOR-PROFIT CAMPAIGN HAS RUN FOR THREE
YEARS IN NEW YORK CITY SUBWAYS.

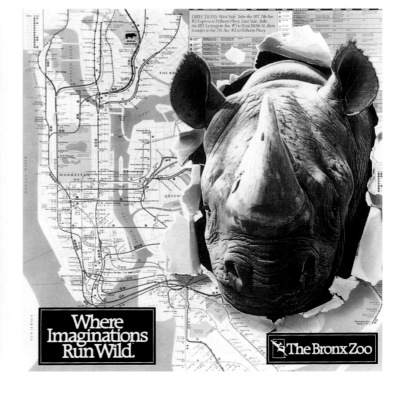

EVENT ZOOFARI '93
DESCRIPTION OF PIECE(S) POSTER
DESIGN FIRM BARTELS & COMPANY, INC.
ART DIRECTOR DAVID BARTELS
DESIGNER BRIAN BARCLAY
ILLUSTRATOR BRALDT BRALDS

THIS AWARD-WINNING POSTER PROMOTED
A ST. LOUIS MAJOR FUNDRAISING EVENT
FOR THE ST. LOUIS ZOO.

EVENT ZOOFARI
DESCRIPTION OF PIECE(S) POSTER
DESIGN FIRM BARTELS & COMPANY, INC.
ART DIRECTOR DAVID BARTELS
DESIGNER MARYBETH BRISTOW, BRIAN BARCLAY
ILLUSTRATOR BRALDT BRALDS

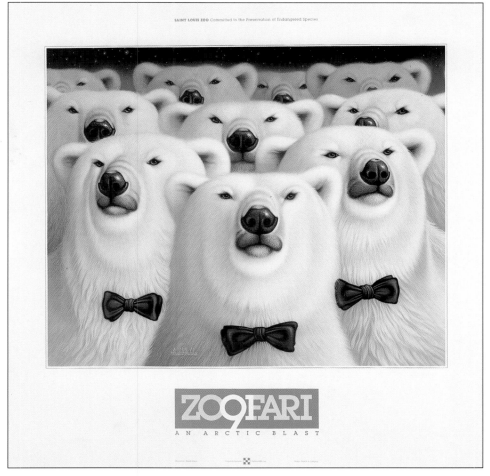

CLOCKWISE FROM TOP LEFT

EVENT "SUPERHERO TO ANTIHERO: COMIC BOOK ART IN THE 1960S"/
NEW YORK ART DIRECTORS CLUB SPEAKER LUNCHEON SERIES
DESCRIPTION OF PIECE(S) INVITATION
DESIGN FIRM THE DYNAMIC DUO, INC.
ART DIRECTOR ARLEN SCHUMER
DESIGNER ARLEN SCHUMER
ILLUSTRATOR ARLEN SCHUMER (DRAWING), SHERRI WOLFGANG (COLOR ART)

ART BASED ON ACTUAL COMIC BOOK PANEL BY DC COMICS.

EVENT "INANIMATE ANUMALS"
DESCRIPTION OF PIECE(S) POSTER
DESIGN FIRM SACKETT DESIGN ASSOCIATES
ART DIRECTOR MARK SACKETT
DESIGNER MARK SACKETT, WAYNE SAKAMOTO
ILLUSTRATOR KIM HOWARD

PROMOTION FOR THE CALIFORNIA CRAFTS MUSEUM

EVENT "LADIES WHO LEAD"/FASHION SHOW FOR JUNIOR LEAGUE OF PALO
ALTO AND NEIMAN MARCUS
DESCRIPTION OF PIECE(S) ICONS
DESIGN FIRM BENNETT/ELIA
ART DIRECTOR PEGGY BENNETT, RANDALL ELIA
DESIGNER JOHN EVANS
ILLUSTRATOR JOHN EVANS

WELCOME TO NEW YORK. SEE YOU AT THE TOY FAIR. WE'LL BE IN SHOWROOM #1204-1206, 1107 BROADWAY. **ERECTOR**

EVENT TOY FAIR
DESCRIPTION OF PIECE(S) ERECTOR CITY
DESIGN FIRM MVBMS
ART DIRECTOR WALLY AREVALO
ILLUSTRATOR TONY RANDAZZO

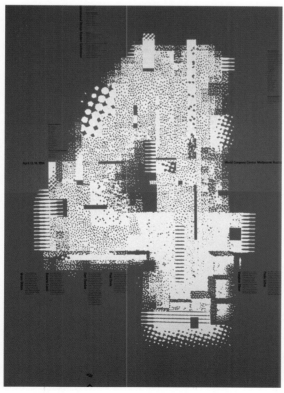

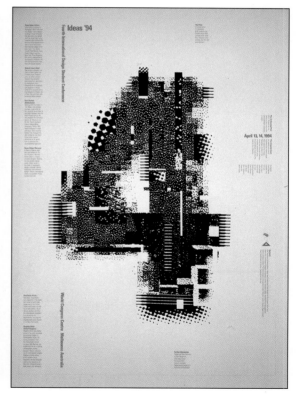

EVENT INTERNATIONAL DESIGN STUDENT CONFERENCE
DESCRIPTION OF PIECE(S) POSTERS
DESIGN FIRM CATO DESIGN INC.
DESIGNER KEN CATO

EVENT "REACH FOR THE STARS"/
ADVERTISING/DESIGN SHOW
DESCRIPTION OF PIECE(S) LETTERHEAD,
SWEATSHIRT, POSTER, AWARD
DESIGN FIRM SAYLES GRAPHIC DESIGN
ART DIRECTOR JOHN SAYLES
DESIGNER JOHN SAYLES

THIS CAMPAIGN MARKED THE 25TH-
ANNIVERSARY ADDY AWARDS IN DES MOINES.

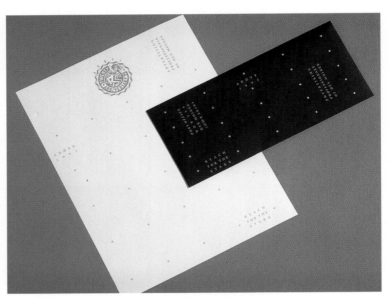

78

FACING PAGES

EVENT NATIVE AMERICAN FILM & MEDIA
CELEBRATION
DESCRIPTION OF PIECE(S) FUNDRAISING/
ADVERTISING MATERIALS PACKAGE
DESIGN FIRM BERNHARDT FUDYMA DESIGN GROUP
ART DIRECTOR CRAIG BERNHARDT,
JANICE FUDYMA
DESIGNER IRIS BROWN, CRAIG BERNHARDT
PHOTOGRAPHER VARIOUS

MOST OF THE COMPONENTS DID NOT UTILIZE STAPLES,
HAD MULTIPLE USES, AND WERE ASSEMBLED BY
MEMBERS OF NATIVE AMERICAN COMMUNITY.

EVENT VIEUX CARRE ANNUAL BENEFIT
DESCRIPTION OF PIECE(S) INVITATION, THANK YOU,
    AUCTION LIST
DESIGN FIRM ADELE BASS & CO. DESIGN
ART DIRECTOR ADELE BASS
DESIGNER ADELE BASS
ILLUSTRATOR ADELE BASS

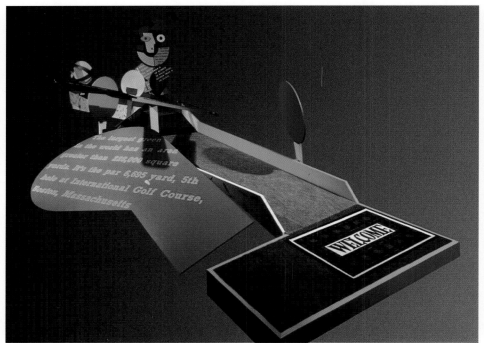

EVENT "STROKES OF GENIUS"/
    GOLF BENEFIT EVENT
DESCRIPTION OF PIECE(S) INVITATION, EXHIBIT
DESIGN FIRM SAYLES GRAPHIC DESIGN
ART DIRECTOR JOHN SAYLES
DESIGNER JOHN SAYLES

CLOCKWISE FROM TOP LEFT

Event Art & Fantasy Art Auction Benefit
Description of Piece(s) Invitation
Art Director Sid Daniels
Designer Sid Daniels
Illustrator Sid Daniels

This art auction benefited the Gay Games IV and Cultural Festival.

Event Alzheimer's Charity Pro Am
Description of Piece(s) Poster
Design Firm SullivanPerkins
Art Director Ron Sullivan
Designer Jon Flaming
Illustrator Jon Flaming

Event "A Demand Performance"/ Dance Performance
Description of Piece(s) Save-the-date card
Design Firm Clarke/Thompson
Art Director Bud Clarke
Designer Bud Clarke, Sid Daniels
Illustrator Sid Daniels

The greatest names in dance and fashion design unite to benefit The Design Industries Foundation for Aids.

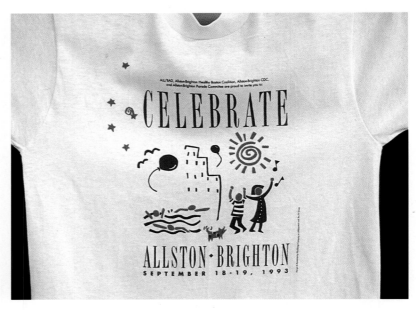

EVENT MARCH OF DIMES WALK AMERICA CAMPAIGN
DESCRIPTION OF PIECE(S) T-SHIRT, BUTTON
DESIGN FIRM THE DESIGN COMPANY
ART DIRECTOR BUSHA HUSAK
DESIGNER BUSHA HUSAK
ILLUSTRATOR BUSHA HUSAK

EVENT CELEBRATE ALLSTON-BRIGHTON
DESCRIPTION OF PIECE(S) T-SHIRT
DESIGN FIRM THE DESIGN COMPANY
ART DIRECTOR BUSHA HUSAK
DESIGNER BUSHA HUSAK
ILLUSTRATOR BUSHA HUSAK

EVENT MARCH OF DIMES WALK-A-THON
DESCRIPTION OF PIECE(S) POSTER
DESIGN FIRM SULLIVANPERKINS
ART DIRECTOR RON SULLIVAN, LORRAINE CHARMAN
DESIGNER LORRAINE CHARMAN
PHOTOGRAPHER ROBB DEBENPORT
COPYWRITER DAVY WOODRUFF

Have a Heart, Take the Walk

FIGHT AIDS

NEW MEXICO AIDS WALK 1993

C I A O D O W N

an evening of Italian foods and festivities

The 1991 Cystic Fibrosis Celebrity Waiters Night

CLOCKWISE FROM TOP LEFT

Event AIDS Walk
Description of Piece(s) Poster
Design Firm Vaughn Wedeen Creative
Art Director Rick Vaughn
Designer Lisa Graff
Illustrator Lisa Graff

Event "Ciao Down"/Fundraiser Dinner
Description of Piece(s) Poster
Design Firm Vaughn Wedeen Creative
Art Director Steve Wedeen
Designer Steve Wedeen

Pro bono poster for Cystic Fibrosis Foundation.

Event "AIDS/HIV Life Center"
Description of Piece(s) Valentine invitation
Design Firm Sackett Design Associates
Art Director Mark Sackett
Designer Mark Sackett, Wayne Sakamoto

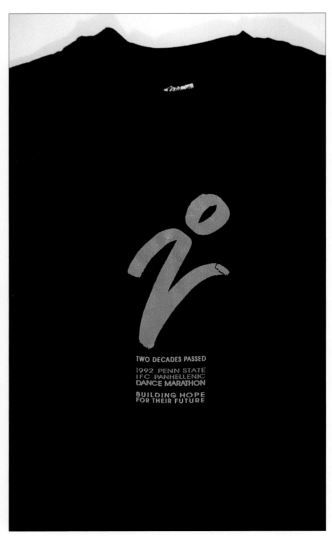

CLOCKWISE FROM TOP LEFT

Event "Dine With Us!"/Fundraiser Dinner
Description of Piece(s) Poster
Design Firm Vaughn Wedeen Creative
Art Director Rick Vaughn
Designer Rick Vaughn
Illustrator Rick Vaughn

Event 20th Annual Dance Marathon
Description of Piece(s) T-shirt
Design Firm Sommese Design
Art Director Kristin Sommese
Designer Jim Lilly

Annual student event raises over $1 million each year for children with cancer.

Event "Topping the Charts" Party/Huntington Banks United Way Campaign
Description of Piece(s) Incentive gift box, box tag, annoucement "record", letterhead
Design Firm Rickabaugh Graphics
Art Director Eric Rickabaugh
Designer Tina Zientarski
Illustrator Michael Linley

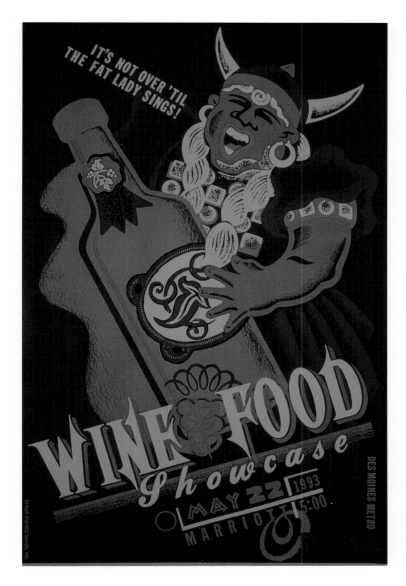

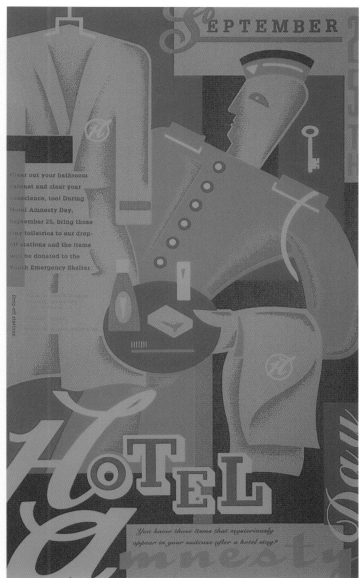

CLOCKWISE FROM TOP LEFT

EVENT "WINE & FOOD SHOWCASE"
DESCRIPTION OF PIECE(S) POSTER
DESIGN FIRM SAYLES GRAPHIC DESIGN
ART DIRECTOR JOHN SAYLES
DESIGNER JOHN SAYLES

THIS EVENT WAS A BENEFIT FOR A LOCAL OPERA.

EVENT "HOTEL AMNESTY DAY"
DESCRIPTION OF PIECE(S) POSTER
DESIGN FIRM SAYLES GRAPHIC DESIGN
ART DIRECTOR JOHN SAYLES
DESIGNER JOHN SAYLES

THIS FUNDRAISING EVENT ALLOWED DONORS TO
GIVE ITEMS "BORROWED" FROM HOTELS.

EVENT "MARCH OF DIMES BID FOR BACHELORS"
DESCRIPTION OF PIECE(S) POSTER,
BROCHURE, TICKETS
DESIGN FIRM SACKETT DESIGN ASSOCIATES
ART DIRECTOR MARK SACKETT
DESIGNER MARK SACKETT, WAYNE SAKAMOTO
ILLUSTRATOR MARK SACKETT,
WAYNE SAKAMOTO

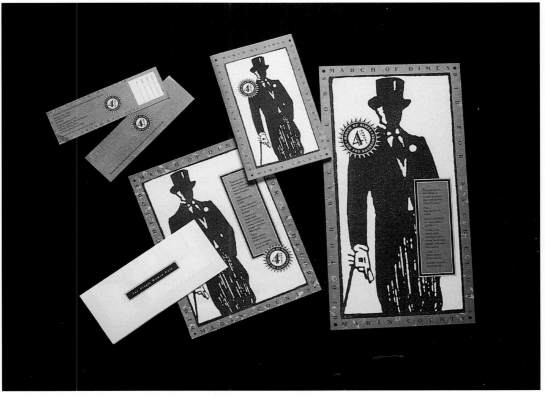

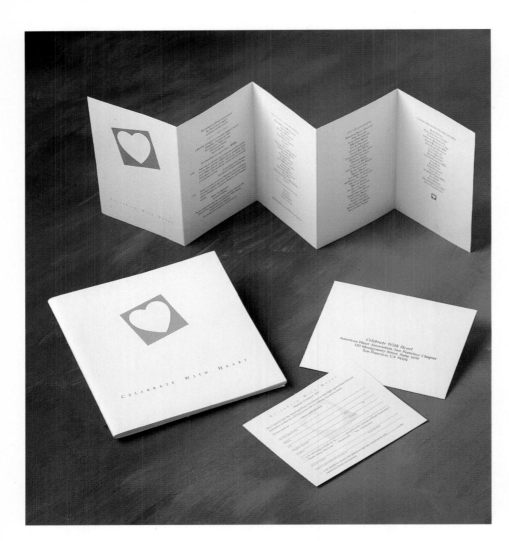

CLOCKWISE FROM LEFT

EVENT CELEBRATE WITH HEART WINE AUCTION
DESCRIPTION OF PIECE(S) PROGRAM COVER
DESIGN FIRM DAN FRAZIER DESIGN
ART DIRECTOR DAN FRAZIER
DESIGNER DAN FRAZIER
ILLUSTRATOR DAN FRAZIER

EVENT SY BARASH REGATTA
DESCRIPTION OF PIECE(S) LOGO, T-SHIRT
DESIGN FIRM SOMMESE DESIGN
ART DIRECTOR KRISTIN SOMMESE
DESIGNER KRISTIN SOMMESE
PHOTOGRAPHER KRISTIN SOMMESE

A DAY-LONG PERFORMANCE BY VARIOUS ROCK GROUPS BENEFITS THE AMERICAN CANCER SOCIETY.

EVENT WOMEN'S AWARENESS WEEK
DESCRIPTION OF PIECE(S) LOGO
DESIGN FIRM SOMMESE DESIGN
ART DIRECTOR KRISTIN SOMMESE
DESIGNER KIRSTIN SOMMESE

EVENT WOMEN'S AWARENESS WEEK
DESCRIPTION OF PIECE(S) LOGO
DESIGN FIRM SOMMESE DESIGN
ART DIRECTOR KRISTIN SOMMESE
DESIGNER KRISTIN SOMMESE

EVENT IDAHO HUMANE SOCIETY'S THIRD ANNUAL BACKYARD PARTY
DESCRIPTION OF PIECE(S) INVITATION (2-COLOR)
DESIGN FIRM CHRIS BLAKEMAN DESIGN
ART DIRECTOR CHRIS BLAKEMAN
DESIGNER CHRIS BLAKEMAN

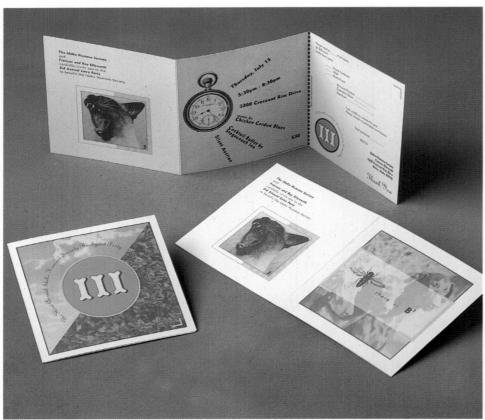

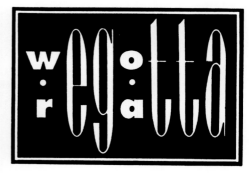

EVENT JUST SAY "NO" TENNIS TOURNAMENT
DESCRIPTION OF PIECE(S) T-SHIRT SERIES
DESIGN FIRM DAN FRAZIER DESIGN
ART DIRECTOR DAN FRAZIER
DESIGNER DAN FRAZIER
ILLUSTRATOR DAN FRAZIER

EVENT "A GENEROUS HELPING"/
     BENEFIT DINNER
DESCRIPTION OF PIECE(S) INVITATION
DESIGN FIRM SAYLES GRAPHIC DESIGN
ART DIRECTOR JOHN SAYLES
DESIGNER JOHN SAYLES

SCREENPRINTED ON A LINEN NAPKIN, THIS
INVITATION WAS MAILED IN A BOX.

EVENT RUN FOR THE ZOO
DESCRIPTION OF PIECE(S) POSTER
DESIGN FIRM VAUGHN WEDEEN CREATIVE
ART DIRECTOR STEVE WEDEEN
DESIGNER STEVE WEDEEN
ILLUSTRATOR KEVIN TOLMAN

SPORTING EVENTS

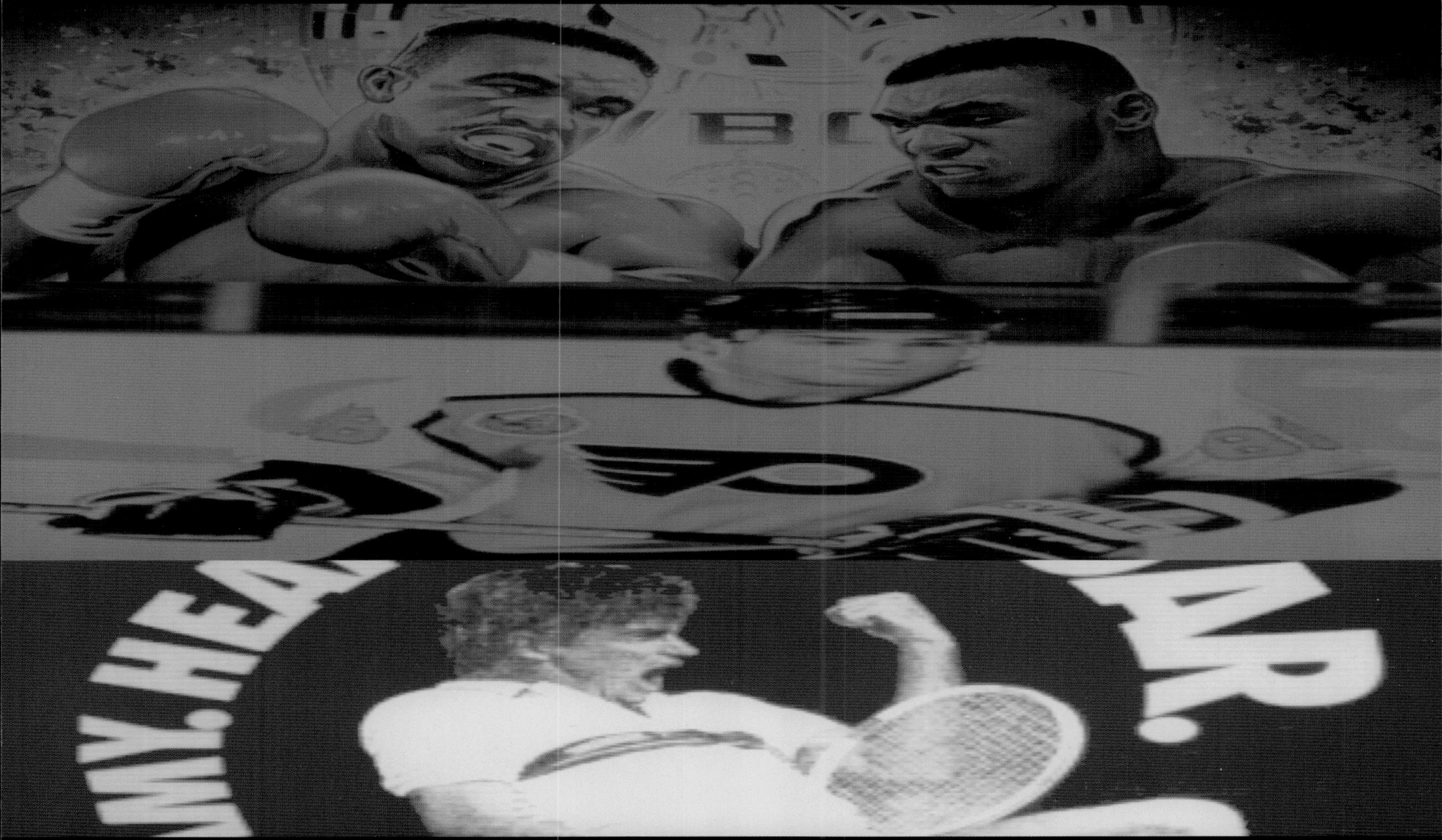

Event Duke City Marathon
Description of Piece(s) Poster, T-shirt, awards
Design Firm Vaughn Wedeen Creative
Art Director Rick Vaughn
Designer Rick Vaughn
Illustrator Rick Vaughn

EVENT Duke City Marathon
DESCRIPTION OF PIECE(S) Poster, T-shirt, awards
DESIGN FIRM Vaughn Wedeen Creative
ART DIRECTOR Rick Vaughn
DESIGNER Rick Vaughn
ILLUSTRATOR Rick Vaughn

EVENT 1993 MYKLEBUST BROCKMAN GOLF OPEN
DESCRIPTION OF PIECE(S) LOGO, T-SHIRT, GOLF BAG,
  TICKETS, INVITATION
DESIGN FIRM MYKLEBUST BROCKMAN INC.
ART DIRECTOR CHRISTOPHER BUCHEIT
DESIGNER CHRISTOPHER BUCHEIT
ILLUSTRATOR CHRISTOPHER BUCHEIT

PROMOTIONAL ITEMS FOR COMPANY GOLF TOURNAMENT

EVENT AGASSI/MCENROE TENNIS EXHIBITION
DESCRIPTION OF PIECE(S) POSTER
DESIGN FIRM NIKE, INC.
ART DIRECTOR JEFF WEITHMAN
DESIGNER JEFF WEITHMAN

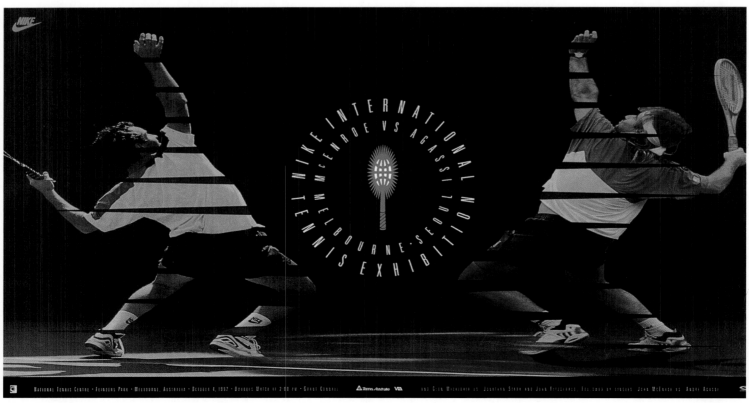

EVENT CORESTATES CHAMPIONSHIP
DESCRIPTION OF PIECE(S) POSTERS, BROCHURES
DESIGN FIRM DOREE LOSCHIAVO STUDIO
ART DIRECTOR DAVID CHAUNER
ILLUSTRATOR DOREE LOSCHIAVO

A L L E Y O O O P H A R A J U K U T O K Y O J A P A N A P R I L 2 7 , 1 9 9 3

EVENT OPENING OF HARAJUKU, JAPAN
DESCRIPTION OF PIECE(S) POSTER
DESIGN FIRM NIKE INC.
ART DIRECTOR JOHN NORMAN
DESIGNER JOHN NORMAN

95

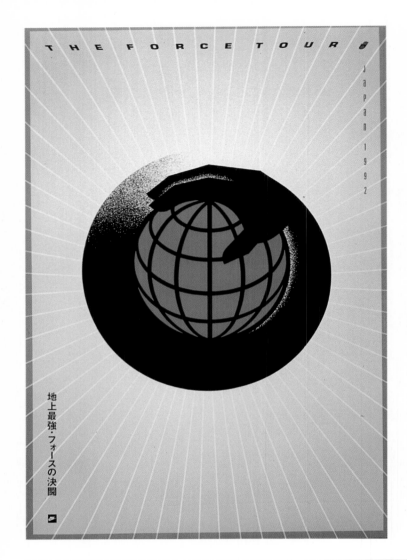

CLOCKWISE FROM TOP LEFT

EVENT NIKE BASKETBALL EXHIBITION, JAPAN
DESCRIPTION OF PIECE(S) POSTER
DESIGN FIRM NIKE INC.
ART DIRECTOR JOHN NORMAN
DESIGNER JOHN NORMAN

EVENT DUKE CITY MARATHON
DESCRIPTION OF PIECE(S) POSTER
DESIGN FIRM VAUGHN WEDEEN CREATIVE
ART DIRECTOR RICK VAUGHN
DESIGNER RICK VAUGHN
ILLUSTRATOR RICK VAUGHN

EVENT OPENING OF NIKETOWN ATLANTA, ORANGE COUNTY
DESCRIPTION OF PIECE(S) SWOOSH INVITATION POSTER
DESIGN FIRM NIKE INC.
ART DIRECTOR CLARK RICHARDSON
DESIGNER CLARK RICHARDSON

EVENT BICYCLE RACE/DUPONT
DESCRIPTION OF PIECE(S) PRESS KIT: LOGO
ON SHIRTS, POSTERS, T-SHIRTS
DESIGN FIRM MIKE QUON DESIGN OFFICE
ART DIRECTOR MIKE QUON, L. STEVENS
DESIGNER MIKE QUON
ILLUSTRATOR MIKE QUON

EVENT MALIBU GRAND PRIX NATIONAL SENIOR CHALLENGE
DESCRIPTION OF PIECE(S) POSTER
DESIGN FIRM RICKABAUGH GRAPHICS
ART DIRECTOR MICHAEL TENNYSON SMITH
DESIGNER MICHAEL TENNYSON SMITH
ILLUSTRATOR MICHAEL TENNYSON SMITH

EVENT CORPORATE CHALLENGE RUNNING RACE
DESCRIPTION OF PIECE(S) T-SHIRT
DESIGN FIRM METROPOLIS, INC.
ART DIRECTOR DENISE MENDELSOHN
DESIGNER LISA MARIE DE SENO
ILLUSTRATOR LISA MARIE DE SENO

EVENT TUCSON POLO CHARITY EVENT
DESCRIPTION OF PIECE(S) POSTER AND COLLATERAL
DESIGN FIRM BOELTS BROS. DESIGN INC.
ART DIRECTOR JACKSON BOELTS, ERIC BOELTS
DESIGNER JACKSON BOELTS, ERIC BOELTS,
KERRY STRATFORD
ILLUSTRATOR JACKSON BOELTS

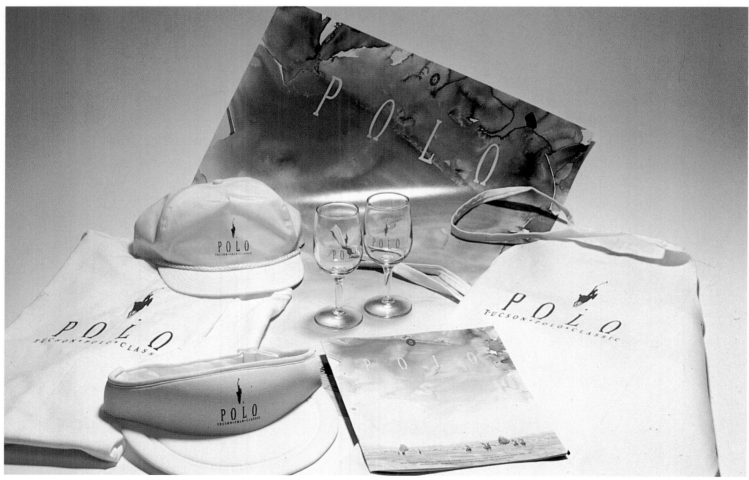

Event Power Play Series
Description of Piece(s) Promotional brochure
Design Firm Target Center
Art Director Brendan J. Finnegan
Designer Scott Kneeskern
Photographer John Bennet Studios

Event featured NHL neutral sight games as well as University of Minnesota and Olympic hockey games.

The Puck Drops Here.

POWERPLAY SERIES

Announcing The Power Play Series At Target Center.

TARGET ⊙ CENTER

Event 58TH COTTON BOWL CLASSICS
Description of Piece(s) INVITATION PACKAGE,
  TICKETS
Design Firm BALCOM CANTRELL ADVERTISING
Photographer JAMES SMITH

Event 58TH COTTON BOWL CLASSICS
Description of Piece(s) GAME TICKET, PROGRAM,
  MEDIA GUIDE
Design Firm BALCOM CANTRELL ADVERTSING
Photographer JAMES SMITH

EVENT DENVER NUGGETS SEASON
DESCRIPTION OF PIECE(S) SEASON TICKETS
DESIGN FIRM DENVER NUGGETS
ART DIRECTOR DAN PRICE
DESIGNER MICHAEL BEINDORFF

EVENT MINNESOTA TIMBERWOLVES/
NBA BASKETBALL TEAM
DESCRIPTION OF PIECE(S) MEDIA GUIDE
DESIGN FIRM TARGET CENTER
ART DIRECTOR BRENDAN J. FINNEGAN
DESIGNER SCOTT KNEESKERN
PHOTOGRAPHER WILLIAM RIDEG

EVENT TUCSON POLO EVENT
DESCRIPTION OF PIECE(S) POSTER AND COLLATERAL
DESIGN FIRM BOELTS BROS. DESIGN INC.
ART DIRECTOR JACKSON BOELTS, ERIC BOELTS
DESIGNER JACKSON BOELTS, ERIC BOELTS,
    KERRY STRATFORD
ILLUSTRATOR ERIC BOELTS

CLOCKWISE FROM TOP LEFT

EVENT MARLBORO HORSE RACE
DESCRIPTION OF PIECE(S) POSTER
DESIGN FIRM MIKE QUON DESIGN OFFICE
ART DIRECTOR ALAN MOGEL
DESIGNER MIKE QUON
ILLUSTRATOR MIKE QUON

EVENT WHITE ROCK MARATHON
DESCRIPTION OF PIECE(S) POSTER
DESIGN FIRM SIBLEY/PETEET
ART DIRECTOR JOHN EVANS
DESIGNER JOHN EVANS
ILLUSTRATOR JOHN EVANS

EVENT CHICAGO SUN TIMES TRIATHLON
DESCRIPTION OF PIECE(S) LOGO
DESIGN FIRM JIM LANGE DESIGN
ART DIRECTOR JAN LANGE
DESIGNER JIM LANGE
ILLUSTRATOR JIM LANGE

Event Annual Charity Polo Event
Description of Piece(s) Poster
Design Firm Boelts Bros. Design Inc.
Art Director Jackson Boelts, Eric Boelts
Designer Jackson Boelts, Eric Boelts
Illustrator Eric Boelts

Event Annual Charity Polo Event
Description of Piece(s) Poster
Design Firm Boelts Bros Design Inc.
Art Director Jackson Boelts, Eric Boelts
Designer Jackson Boelts, Eric Boelts
Illustrator Jackson Boelts

EVENT ANNUAL CHARITY POLO EVENT
DESCRIPTION OF PIECE(S) POSTER
DESIGN FIRM BOELTS BROS. DESIGN INC.
ART DIRECTOR JACKSON BOELTS, ERIC BOELTS
DESIGNER JACKSON BOELTS, ERIC BOELTS
ILLUSTRATOR JACKSON BOELTS

Event Canned Food Invitational Swim Meet
Description of Piece(s) Invitation
Design Firm Dan Frazier Design
Art Director Dan Frazier
Designer Dan Frazier
Illustrator Dan Frazier

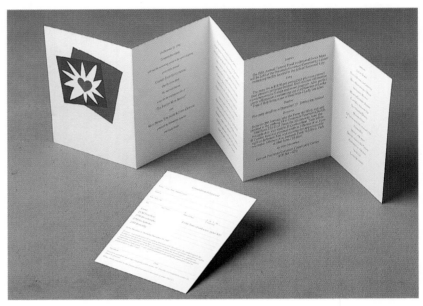

Event Canned Food Invitational Swim Meet
Description of Piece(s) T-shirt
Design Firm Dan Frazier Design
Art Director Dan Frazier
Designer Dan Frazier
Illustrator Dan Frazier

Special Olympics World Games

CONNECTICUT 1995

Sport. Spirit. Splendor. July 1-9

REUNION
At Riverfront

SKATERS'
CHAMPIONSHIPS

RIVERFRONT COLISEUM APRIL 3-5, 1992 CINCINNATI · USA

CLOCKWISE FROM TOP LEFT

EVENT SPECIAL OLYMPICS WORLD GAMES
DESCRIPTION OF PIECE(S) POSTER
DESIGN FIRM OSTRO DESIGN
ART DIRECTOR MICHAEL OSTRO
DESIGNER MICHAEL OSTRO
ILLUSTRATOR MICHAEL OSTRO

THIS WILL BE THE SINGLE LARGEST SPORTING
EVENT IN THE WORLD IN 1995.

EVENT SKATERS' CHAMPIONSHIPS REUNION
DESCRIPTION OF PIECE(S) POSTER
DESIGN FIRM DESIGNCENTRE OF CINCINNATI
ART DIRECTOR JIM MAKSTALLER
DESIGNER LORI DUEBBER ROBERTSON
ILLUSTRATOR MARY JO RECKER

EVENT TURTLE CREEK RUN
DESCRIPTION OF PIECE(S) LOGO
DESIGN FIRM SIBLEY/PETEET
ART DIRECTOR JOHN EVANS
DESIGNER JOHN EVANS
ILLUSTRATOR JOHN EVANS

EVENT SAILBOAT REGATTA/
OUTDOOR SPORTING EVENTS
DESCRIPTION OF PIECE(S) T-SHIRT
DESIGN FIRM GOGOOP, INC.
ILLUSTRATOR ALYCE K. SANTORO

107

EVENT ARIZONA VOLLEYBALL
DESCRIPTION OF PIECE(S) ILLUSTRATION FOR PROMO PIECES
DESIGN FIRM RPM
DESIGNER JOHN D. SECKMAN JR.
ILLUSTRATOR JOHN D. SECKMAN JR.

EVENT US OPEN/CITIBANK BANNER
DESCRIPTION OF PIECE(S) POSTER
DESIGN FIRM MIKE QUON DESIGN OFFICE
ART DIRECTOR MIKE QUON
DESIGNER MIKE QUON
ILLUSTRATOR MIKE QUON

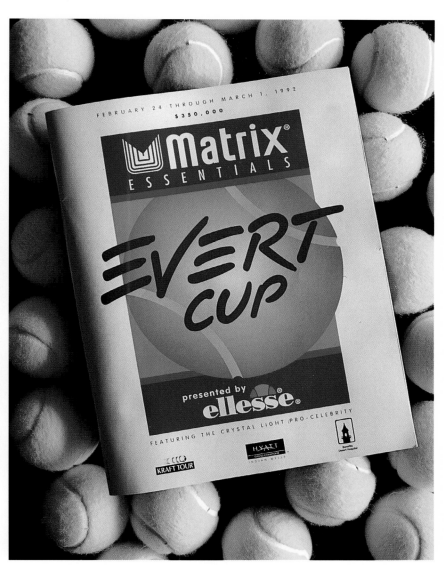

EVENT EVERT CUP/PROFESSIONAL TENNIS
TOURNAMENT (WTA TOUR)
DESCRIPTION OF PIECE(S) PROGRAM COVER,
APPAREL, STATIONERY, EVENT SIGNAGE
DESIGN FIRM MARK PALMER DESIGN
ART DIRECTOR MARK PALMER
DESIGNER MARK PALMER

PROFESSIONAL TENNIS TOURNAMENT (WTA TOUR).

EVENT CANNED FOOD INVITATIONAL SWIM MEET
DESCRIPTION OF PIECE(S) PROGRAM COVER
DESIGN FIRM DAN FRAZIER DESIGN
ART DIRECTOR DAN FRAZIER
DESIGNER DAN FRAZIER
ILLUSTRATOR DAN FRAZIER

EVENT SHOOT OUT
DESCRIPTION OF PIECE(S) POSTER
DESIGN FIRM SULLIVANPERKINS
ART DIRECTOR ART GARCIA
DESIGNER ART GARCIA

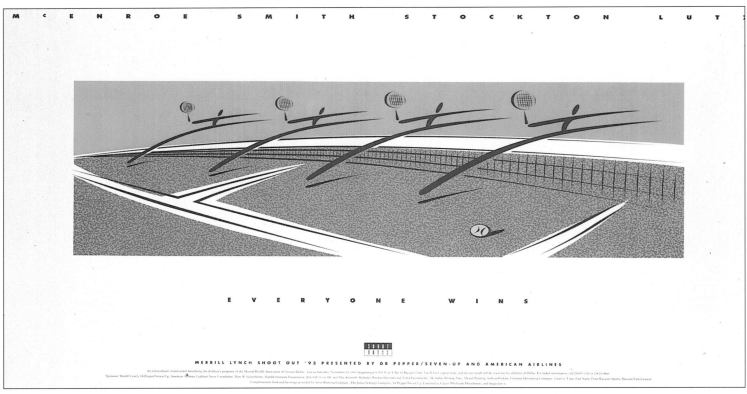

HE IS JIMMY. HEAR HIM ROAR.

In case you haven't heard, Merrill Lynch Shoot Out '92

is a tennis exhibition that benefits the children's programs of the

Mental Health Association of Greater Dallas.

Join us Monday, November 16, beginning at 6 P.M., at

1 Bar M Racquet Club with tennis greats

Jimmy Connors, Dick Stockton, Anne Smith, and JoAnne Russell.

Call MHA at 871.2420 or 233.4444 for ticket information.

EVENT MENTAL HEALTH ASSOCIATION SHOOT OUT
DESCRIPTION OF PIECE(S) POSTER
DESIGN FIRM SullivanPerkins
ART DIRECTOR ART GARCIA
DESIGNER SHAUN MARSHALL
ILLUSTRATOR SHAUN MARSHALL

EVENT WORLD WRESTLING FEDERATION
    SURVIVOR SERIES
DESCRIPTION OF PIECE(S) T-SHIRT
DESIGN FIRM CREATIVE SERVICES/TITAN
    SPORTS, INC.
ART DIRECTOR ADRIANA WECHSLER
CREATIVE DIRECTOR DEBBIE CYRGALIS
ILLUSTRATOR TOM FLEMMING

EVENT DAVIS CUP SEMI-FINALS
DESCRIPTION OF PIECE(S) TICKET
DESIGN FIRM TARGET CENTER
ART DIRECTOR BRENDAN J. FINNEGAN
DESIGNER BRENDAN J. FINNEGAN

INTERNATIONAL TEAM TENNIS EVENT
FEATURED TEAM USA VERSUS TEAM SWEDEN.

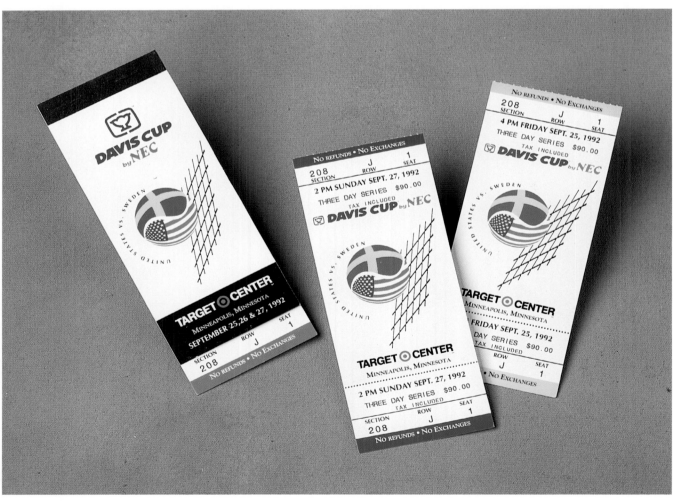

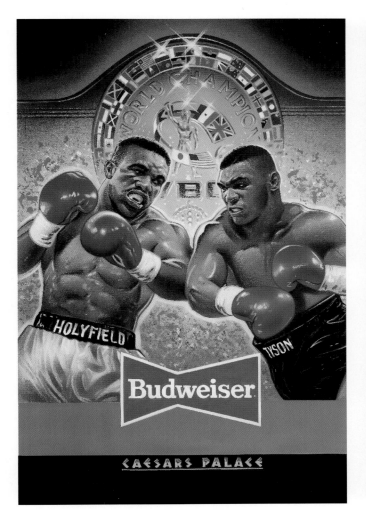

EVENT TYSON-HOLYFIELD FIGHT
DESCRIPTION OF PIECE(S) POSTER
DESIGN FIRM KREPS-WISE
ILLUSTRATOR GARY CICCARELLI

EVENT WORLD WRESTLING FEDERATION
KING OF THE RING
DESCRIPTION OF PIECE(S) POSTER
DESIGN FIRM CREATIVE SERVICES/
TITAN SPORTS, INC.
ART DIRECTOR KEVIN MAY
CREATIVE DIRECTOR DEBBIE CYRGALIS
DESIGNER KEVIN MAY, RON MELLEN (LOGO)
ILLUSTRATOR KEVIN MAY, RON MELLEN (LOGO)
PHOTOGRAPHER STEVE TAYLOR

EVENT WORLD WRESTLING
FEDERATION WRESTLEMANIA IV
DESCRIPTION OF PIECE(S) T-SHIRT
DESIGN FIRM CREATIVE SERVICES/
TITAN SPORTS, INC.
CREATIVE DIRECTOR DEBBIE CYRGALIS
DESIGNER PAUL MAGLIARI
ILLUSTRATOR PAUL MAGLIARI

EVENT BOSTON CELTICS BASKETBALL
DESCRIPTION OF PIECE(S) MEDIA GUIDE (COVER)
ART DIRECTOR DAVE ZUCCARRO
ILLUSTRATOR BOT RODA

EVENT LOS ANGELES LAKERS BASKETBALL
DESCRIPTION OF PIECE(S) MEDIA GUIDE
ART DIRECTOR JOHN BLACK
ILLUSTRATOR BOT RODA

EVENT ATP TENNIS TOURNAMENT
DESCRIPTION OF PIECE(S) POSTER
DESIGN FIRM BRUCE DESIGN
DESIGNER ANNETTE ROSS/BRUCE DESIGN
ILLUSTRATOR ANGIE FISHER/PHOTONICS GRAPHICS
PHOTOGRAPHER MCHALE STUDIOS

Event President's Club
Description of Piece(s) Various
Design Firm Vaughn Wedeen Creative
Art Director Steve Wedeen
Designer Steve Wedeen

The theme for this conference was "Mission Possible"

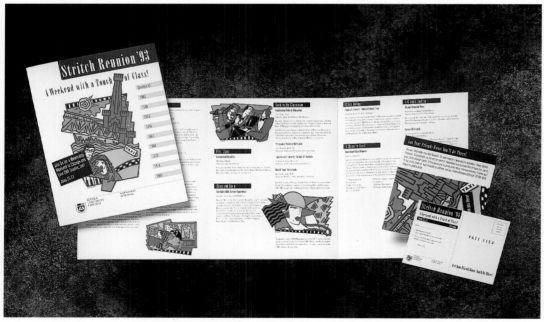

Event Stritch Reunion Loyola University Chicago Medical School
Description of Piece(s) Reunion Package
Design Firm Hafeman Design Group Inc.
Art Director William Hafeman
Designer Tom Carr
Illustrator Maria Strosser

This package was directed to spouses of attendees and emphasized Chicago's restaurants and nightlife.

Event Communication Artists of New
Mexico Meeting/Featured Speakers:
Vaughn Wedeen Creative
Description of Piece(s) Poster
Design Firm Vaughn Wedeen Creative
Art Director Steve Wedeen, Rick Vaughn
Designer Steve Wedeen, Rick Vaughn
Illustrator Rick Vaughn

Event Burlington Resources Executive Symposium
Description of Piece(s) Southwest resort montage
Design Firm Howard Miller and Associates Inc.
Art Director Howard Miller
Designer Jim Starr
Illustrator Jim Starr

117

EVENT IMAGE FACTOR/GRAND OPENING
    CELEBRATION
DESCRIPTION OF PIECE(S) CD LOOK-ALIKE,
    INVITATION
DESIGN FIRM AL PEREZ ILLUSTRATION & DESIGN
DESIGNER AL PEREZ

CLIENT RECEIVED MANY COMPLIMENTS AND CREATIVE
RSVP RESPONSES.

EVENT JANUARY GIFT SHOW
DESCRIPTION OF PIECE(S) DIRECT MAIL
DESIGN FIRM SEGURA INC.
ART DIRECTOR CARLOS SEGURA
DESIGNER CARLOS SEGURA

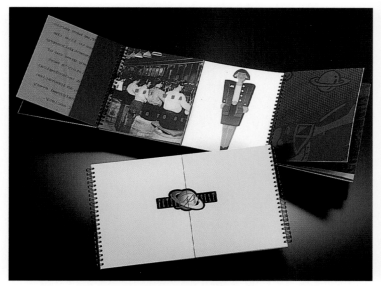

CLOCKWISE FROM TOP LEFT

EVENT 1993 PRESIDENT'S CLUB
DESCRIPTION OF PIECE(S) GUIDE BOOK
DESIGN FIRM VAUGHN WEDEEN CREATIVE
ART DIRECTOR STEVE WEDEEN
DESIGNER STEVE WEDEEN

THIS PIECE WAS FINAL GIFT
GIVEN AT CONFERENCE.

EVENT PRESIDENT'S CLUB
DESCRIPTION OF PIECE(S) CRYSTAL BALL
DESIGN FIRM VAUGHN WEDEEN CREATIVE
ART DIRECTOR STEVE WEDEEN
DESIGNER STEVE WEDEEN
ILLUSTRATOR STEVE WEDEEN, CHIP WYLY

THIS GIFT GIVEN AT THE BEGINNING
OF CONFERENCE REFLECTED
THEME: "FUTURE PRESENT."

EVENT PRESIDENT'S CLUB
DESCRIPTION OF PIECE(S) PRE-ARRIVAL KIT
DESIGN FIRM VAUGHN WEDEEN CREATIVE
ART DIRECTOR RICK VAUGHN
DESIGNER RICK VAUGHN
ILLUSTRATOR KEVIN TOLMAN, CHIP WYLY,
RICK VAUGHN

FACING PAGES

EVENT "BOLDLY INTO TOMORROW"/FOOD
 SERVICES OF AMERICA CONFERENCE
DESCRIPTION OF PIECE(S) INVITATION, EXHIBIT
DESIGN FIRM HORNALL ANDERSON DESIGN
 WORKS
ART DIRECTOR JACK ANDERSON
DESIGNER JACK ANDERSON, JANI DREWFS,
 CLIFF CHUNG, BRIAN O'NEILL

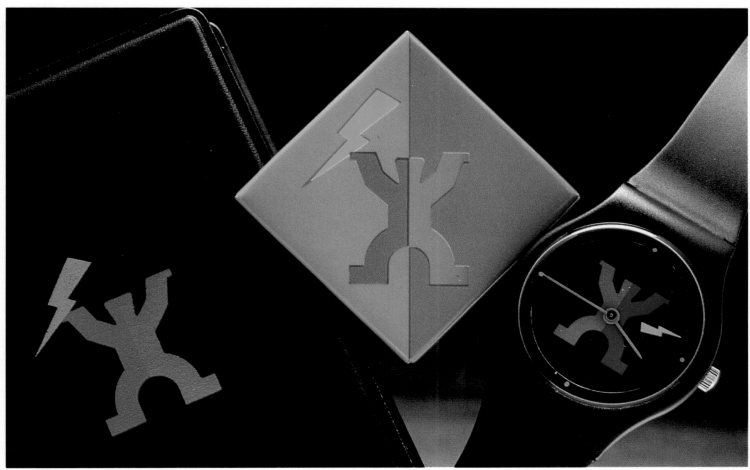

Event "Boldly Into Tomorrow"/Food Services of America Conference
Description of Piece(s) Invitation, exhibit
Design Firm Hornall Anderson Design Works
Art Director Jack Anderson
Designer Jack Anderson, Jani Drewfs, Cliff Chung, Brian O'Neill

Event "Power in Partnership"/Food Services of America Conference
Description of Piece(s) Conference signage
Design Firm Hornall Anderson Design Works
Art Director Jack Anderson
Designer Jack Anderson, Cliff Chung, Scott Eggers, David Bates

EVENT "POWER IN PARTNERSHIP"/FOOD
SERVICES OF AMERICA CONFERENCE
DESCRIPTION OF PIECE(S) CONFERENCE SIGNAGE
DESIGN FIRM HORNALL ANDERSON
DESIGN WORKS
ART DIRECTOR JACK ANDERSON
DESIGNER JACK ANDERSON, CLIFF CHUNG,
SCOTT EGGERS, DAVID BATES

Event Motorolla Awards Night
Description of Piece(s) Invitation, Award
Design Firm Jon Flaming Design
Art Director Didi Stuart
Designer John Evans/ John Evans Design
Illustrator John Evans
Agency Sicola/Martin

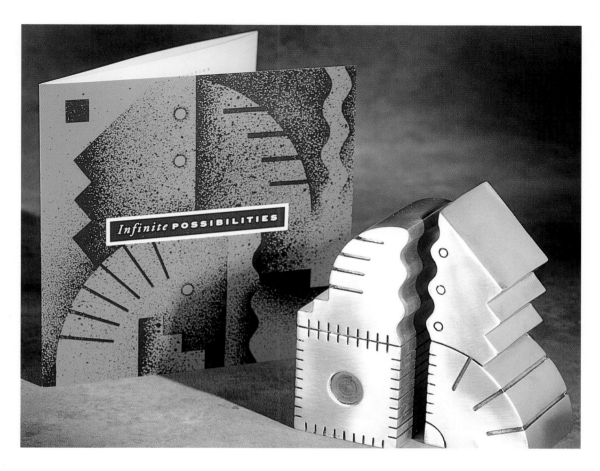

Event "A Time of Change"/ Financial Seminar
Description of Piece(s) Mailer and collateral
Design Firm Sayles Graphic Design
Art Director John Sayles
Designer John Sayles

EVENT DANCE CELEBRATION
DESCRIPTION OF PIECE(S) POSTER
DESIGN FIRM TOKYU AGENCY INC.
ART DIRECTOR RYOICHI KANEDA
DESIGNER RYOICHI KANEDA
ILLUSTRATOR SID DANIELS
PHOTOGRAPHER MASATO YAMADA

TO CELEBRATE THE OPENING OF THE SPRING
COLLECTIONS AT TOKYU DEPARTMENT STORES IN
TOKYO, A SERIES OF WEEKLY DANCES WERE HELD.

EVENT MICROSOFT CORPORATION TECH-ED CONFERENCE
DESCRIPTION OF PIECE(S) CONFERENCE MATERIALS
DESIGN FIRM HORNALL ANDERSON DESIGN WORKS
ART DIRECTOR JACK ANDERSON
DESIGNER JACK ANDERSON, CLIFF CHUNG, DAVID BATES,
   LEO RAYMUNDO, BRIAN O'NEILL
ILLUSTRATOR SCOTT MCDOUGALL, YUTAKA SASAKI
PHOTOGRAPHER TOM MCMACKIN

Event "We've Got the Beat"/
University Event
Description of Piece(s) Poster,
collateral, display
Design Firm Sayles Graphic Design
Art Director John Sayles
Designer John Sayles

Event Association of Research Libraries
Conference on Library Fee-Based Services
Description of Piece(s) Logo
Design Firm Jim Lange Design
Art Director Brigid Welch
Designer Jim Lange
Illustrator Jim Lange

EVENT HARVEST IN THE MARKET
DESCRIPTION OF PIECE(S) POSTER
DESIGN FIRM MULLER & COMPANY
ART DIRECTOR MICHELLE KNAUSS
DESIGNER MICHELLE KNAUSS
ILLUSTRATOR CATHY LAW

EVENT ANGELUS AWARD GALA/ST. VINCENT'S
HOSPITAL & MEDICAL CENTER OF NEW YORK
DESCRIPTION OF PIECE(S) COMMEMORATIVE CALENDAR
DESIGN FIRM THE WYANT GROUP, INC.
ART DIRECTOR JULIA WYANT
DESIGNER JENNIFER DEITZ
ILLUSTRATOR THE WYANT GROUP, INC., JULIE BERSON
PHOTOGRAPHER BILL WESTHEIMER (PORTRAITS)

THIS IS A 15-MONTH CALENDAR WITH AD
SPACES WHICH ARE VISIBLE FOR A WEEK AT A TIME.

EVENT PRESIDENT'S CLUB CRUISE FOR PACESETTER
DESCRIPTION OF PIECE(S) POSTER
DESIGN FIRM NEW IDEA DESIGN INC.
DESIGNER KRISTI MCCLENDON
ILLUSTRATOR RON BOLDT

Event Programart Corporation 25th
   Anniversary
Description of Piece(s) Invitation
   and gifts for employees
Design Firm Carol Lasky Studio
Creative Director Carol Lasky
Designer Erin Donnellan

Event Guggenheim Museum
Description of Piece(s)
   Corporate brochure
Design Firm Guggenheim Museum
Art Director Cara Galowitz
Designer Cara Galowitz
Photographer David Heald (cover)

Right Time Wright Place *Corporate Membership at the Guggenheim*

EVENT CAP FERRAT NOVEMBER MEETING
DESCRIPTION OF PIECE(S) T-SHIRT
DESIGN FIRM METROPOLIS, INC.
ART DIRECTOR DENISE MENDELSOHN
DESIGNER TRINA RISO
ILLUSTRATOR CATHERINE KANNER

THIS ILLUSTRATION WAS
FEATURED ON COVER OF BROCHURE.

EVENT TURNER BROADCASTING
ANNUAL TRUMPET AWARDS
DESCRIPTION OF PIECE(S)
INVITATION, PROGRAM
DESIGN FIRM TWO IN DESIGN
ART DIRECTOR ED PHELPS
DESIGNER ED PHELPS

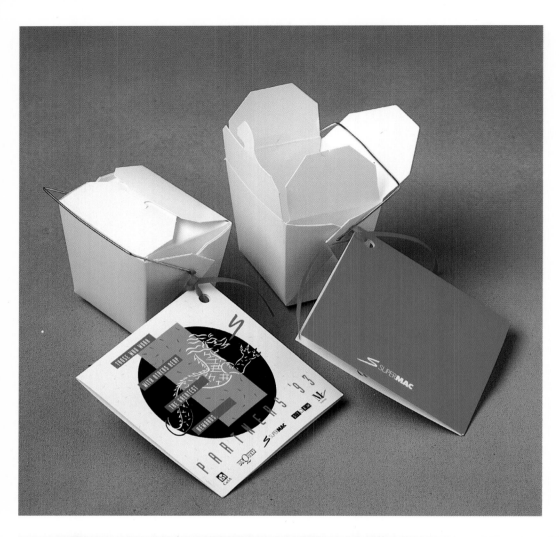

EVENT SUPERMAC DEVELOPER OPEN HOUSE
DESCRIPTION OF PIECE(S) INVITATION
DESIGN FIRM TIRAPELLI DESIGN
ART DIRECTOR LINDA LYDDON
DESIGNER BETH TIRAPELLI
ILLUSTRATOR BETH TIRAPELLI

HIGHLY SUCCESSFUL AND INTRIGUING INVITATION WAS
PROMO PIECE FOR OPEN HOUSE.

EVENT SPEARFISH CREEK CLEAN-UP SPONSORED BY
PIONEER BANK & TRUST, TACO JOHN'S
DESCRIPTION OF PIECE(S) T-SHIRTS
DESIGN FIRM WILD HARE STUDIO
ART DIRECTOR CHUCK EGNACZAK
DESIGNER CHRISTINE PEZEL GRAHAM
ILLUSTRATOR CHRISTINE PEZEL GRAHAM

DESIGNED AND ILLUSTRATED WITH ALDUS FREEHAND

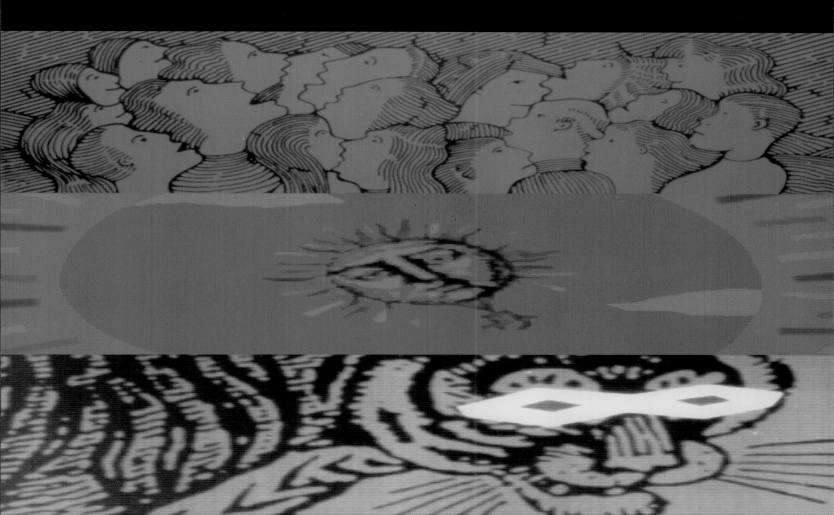

EVENT ANNUAL HALLOWEEN PARTY
DESCRIPTION OF PIECE(S) DAY-OF-THE-DEAD POSTERS
DESIGN FIRM BOELTS BROS. DESIGN INC.
ART DIRECTOR JACKSON BOELTS, ERIC BOELTS
DESIGNER JACKSON BOELTS, ERIC BOELTS,
    KERRY STRATFORD
ILLUSTRATOR ERIC BOELTS

POSTERS ARE SILKSCREENED.

Even "Zoo Boo 4"/Halloween at the Zoo
Description of Piece(s) Poster
Design Firm Vaughn Weeden Creative
Art Director Steve Wedeen
Designer Steve Wedeen

Event "Zoo Boo 3"/Halloween at the Zoo
Description of Piece(s) Poster
Design Firm Vaughn Wedeen Creative
Art Director Steve Wedeen
Designer Steve Wedeen

A Rio Grande Zoo event.

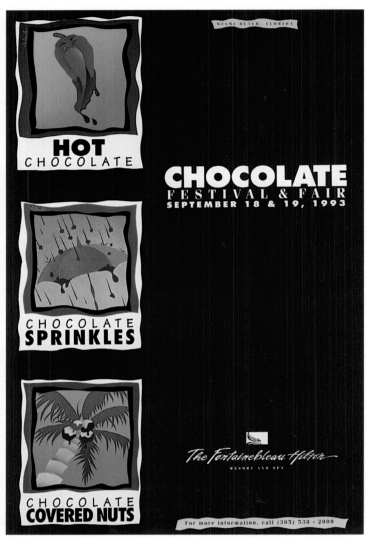

CLOCKWISE FROM TOP LEFT

EVENT CITY FAIR OPENING
DESCRIPTION OF PIECE(S) CAMPAIGN MATERIALS
DESIGN FIRM SULLIVANPERKINS
ART DIRECTOR RON SULLIVAN
DESIGNER LINDA HELTON
ILLUSTRATOR LINDA HELTON

EVENT CHOCOLATE FESTIVAL AND FAIR
DESCRIPTION OF PIECE(S) POSTER
DESIGN FIRM SCHWARTZ AND KAPLAN ADVERTSING
ART DIRECTOR RENEE KUCI
DESIGNER RENEE KUCI
ILLUSTRATOR SID DANIELS

THIS EVENT WAS HELD AT THE FONTAINEBLEAU HILTON RESORT AND SPA IN MIAMI BEACH, FLORIDA.

EVENT 1994 TEJANO CONJUNTO FESTIVAL
DESCRIPTION OF PIECE(S) AIRBRUSH GOAUCHE
COMPUTER SOFTWARE CORELDRAW 4
DESIGNER RICHARD O. MENCHACA
ILLUSTRATOR RICHARD O. MENCHACA
PHOTOGRAPHER ANSEN SEALE

THIS POSTER WAS ENTERED IN THE 13TH ANNUAL STATEWIDE TEJANO CONJUNTO FESTIVAL CONTEST.

EVENT 30TH LEONARD J. WAXDOCK BIRD CALLING CONTEST
DESCRIPTION OF PIECE(S) POSTER
DESIGN FIRM BARTELS & COMPANY, INC.
ART DIRECTOR DAVID BARTELS
DESIGNER BRIAN BARCLAY
ILLUSTRATOR JAMES MARSH

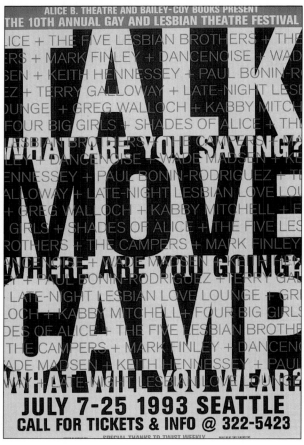

EVENT ASIA SOCIETY IN NEW YORK/
CULTURAL LECTURES FOR KIDS
DESCRIPTION OF PIECE(S) TWO-SIDED POSTER
DESIGN FIRM TARADASH ASSOCIATES
ART DIRECTOR JANET TARADASH, JACK TOM
DESIGNER JACK TOM
ILLUSTRATIONS SHUFU MIYAMOTO (FRONT),
JACK TOM (BACK)

EVENT ALICE B. THEATRE GAY & LESBIAN FESTIVAL
DESCRIPTION OF PIECE(S) TALK, MOVIE, CAMP POSTER
DESIGN FIRM MODERN DOG
ART DIRECTOR VITTORIO COSTARELLA
DESIGNER VITTORIO COSTARELLA

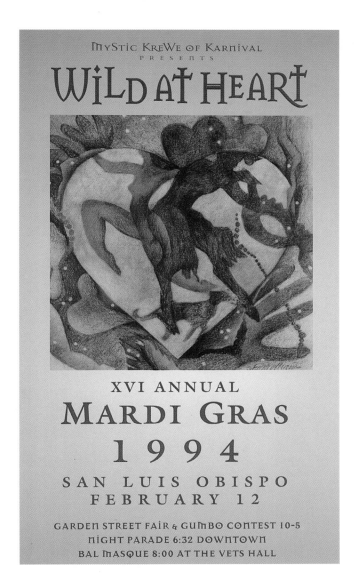

MyStic KreWe of Karnival
PRESENTS

WiLD AT HEART

XVI ANNUAL
MARDI GRAS
1994
SAN LUIS OBISPO
FEBRUARY 12

GARDEN STREET FAIR & GUMBO CONTEST 10-5
NIGHT PARADE 6:32 DOWNTOWN
BAL MASQUE 8:00 AT THE VETS HALL

SEPTEMBER 23, 24 & 25

9TH ANNUAL PLANO

BALLOON FESTIVAL

BOB WOODRUFF PARK

CLOCKWISE FROM TOP LEFT

EVENT MARDI GRAS
DESCRIPTION OF PIECE(S) POSTER
DESIGN FIRM THULÉ DESIGN
DESIGNER MATT THULÉ
ILLUSTRATOR STACEY WILLIAMS

EVENT 9TH ANNUAL PLANO BALLOON FESTIVAL
DESCRIPTION OF PIECE(S) POSTER
DESIGN FIRM SULLIVANPERKINS
ART DIRECTOR RON SULLIVAN
DESIGNER ART GARCIA

EVENT "GROWING-BY DESIGN"/
INTERNATIONAL DESIGN CONFERENCE OF ASPEN
DESCRIPTION OF PIECE(S) POSTER, BROCHURES
DESIGN FIRM THE PUSHPIN GROUP
ART DIRECTOR IVAN CHERMAYEFF,
JANE CLARK CHERMAYEFF
DESIGNER SEYMOUR CHWAST
ILLUSTRATOR SEYMOUR CHWAST

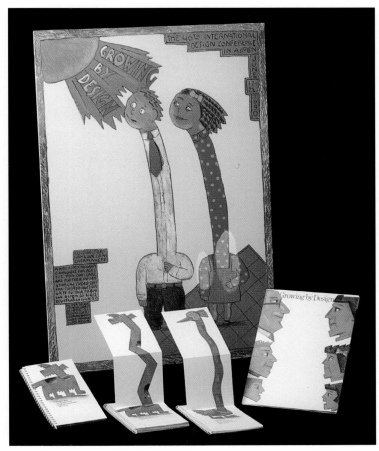

FACING PAGES

Event City of La Quinta 10th Anniversary
Description of Piece(s) Bus shelter, stationery,
    invitation, beverage glass
Design Firm Mark Palmer Design
Art Director Mark Palmer
Designer Mark Palmer

Event Earth Day NYC
Description of Piece(s) Poster
Design Firm The Pushpin Group, Inc.
Art Director Seymour Chwast
Designer Seymour Chwast
Illustrator Seymour Chwast

This design for Earth Day 1991 was
printed on the back of remaining
Earth Day 1990 posters.

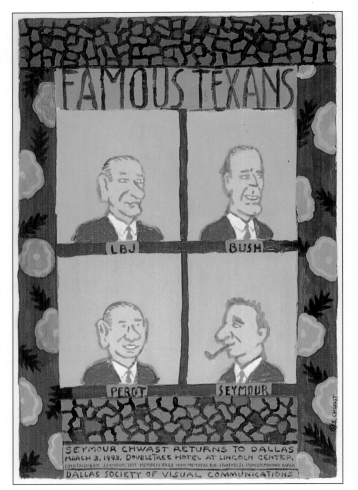

Event "Famous Texans"/Speaking Engagement,
Dallas School of Visual Communication
Description of Piece(s) "Famous Texans" poster
Design Firm The Pushpin Group
Art Director Seymour Chwast
Designer Seymour Chwast
Illustrator Seymour Chwast

EVENT "SANDJAM"/SUMMER EVENT
DESCRIPTION OF PIECE(S) POSTER
DESIGN FIRM SAYLES GRAPHIC DESIGN
ART DIRECTOR JOHN SAYLES
DESIGNER JOHN SAYLES

THIS POSTER PROMOTES A SAND CASTLE
BUILDING CONTEST AMONG ARCHITECTS.

EVENT "SANDJAM '93"/SUMMER EVENT
DESCRIPTION OF PIECE(S) POSTER, T-SHIRT
DESIGN FIRM SAYLES GRAPHIC DESIGN
ART DIRECTOR JOHN SAYLES
DESIGNER JOHN SAYLES

ORIGINALLY POSTPONED DUE TO FLOODING, THE STICKER
VISIBLE ON THE POSTER ANNOUNCES THE RAIN DATE.

Event *"John Sayles Poster Series"*
Description of Piece(s) Posters
Design Firm Sayles Graphic Design
Art Director John Sayles
Designer John Sayles

This series of posters promotes talks
by graphic designer John Sayles.

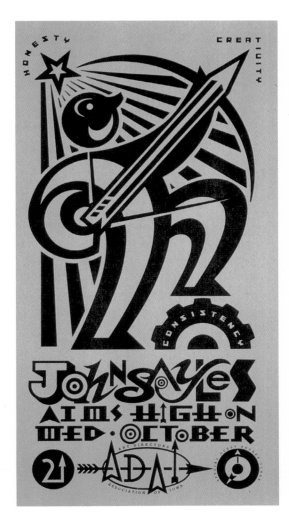

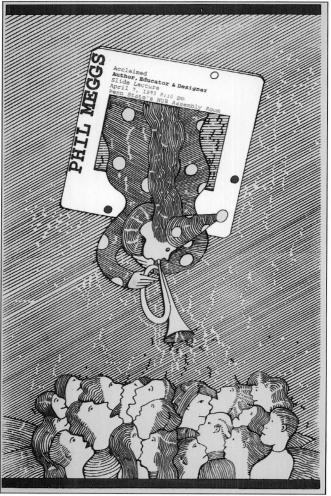

CLOCKWISE FROM TOP LEFT

EVENT LECTURE SERIES
DESCRIPTION OF PIECE(S) POSTER
DESIGN FIRM SOMMESE DESIGN
ART DIRECTOR LANNY SOMMESE
DESIGNER LANNY SOMMESE

LECTURE SERIES WAS MADE UP OF WRITERS
FROM EASTERN EUROPE.

EVENT COSTUME BALL FOR ARCHITECTURE STUDENTS
DESCRIPTION OF PIECE(S) POSTER (SILKSCREEN)
DESIGN FIRM SOMMESE DESIGN
ART DIRECTOR LANNY SOMMESE
DESIGNER LANNY SOMMESE
ILLUSTRATOR LANNY SOMMESE

EVENT PHIL MEGGS LECTURE
DESCRIPTION OF PIECE(S) POSTER (SILKSCREEN)
DESIGN FIRM SOMMESE DESIGN
ART DIRECTOR LANNY SOMMESE
DESIGNER LANNY SOMMESE
ILLUSTRATOR LANNY SOMMESE

LECTURER IS AN EXPERT ON GRAPHIC DESIGN HISTORY.

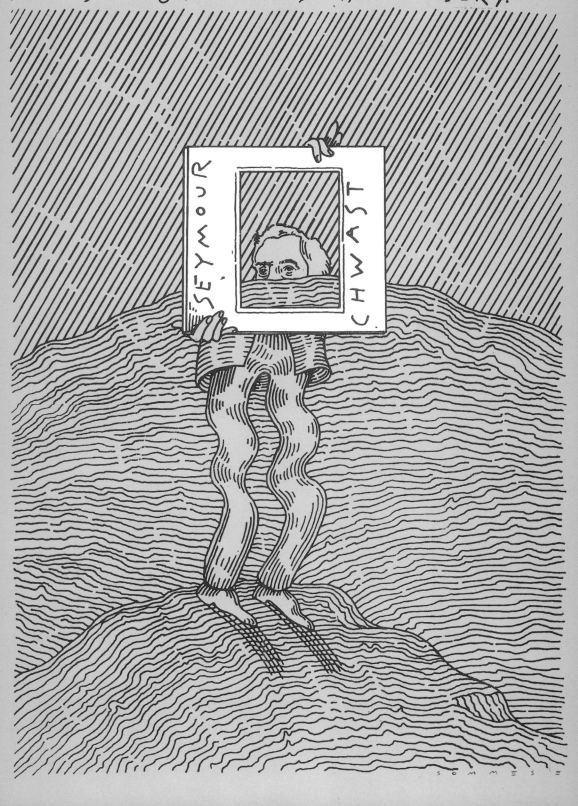

ART DIRECTOR, DESIGNER, ILLUSTRATOR
SLIDE LECTURE KELLER CONFERENCE CENTER,
PENN STATE. 8 P.M. WEDNESDAY, NOVEMBER 7.

SEYMOUR CHWAST

EVENT SEYMOUR CHWAST LECTURE
DESCRIPTION OF PIECE(S) POSTER (SILKSCREEN)
DESIGN FIRM SOMMESE DESIGN
ART DIRECTOR LANNY SOMMESE
DESIGNER LANNY SOMMESE
ILLUSTRATOR LANNY SOMMESE

EVENT "Free For All"/Chemical-Free Party
DESCRIPTION OF PIECE(S) Poster, T-shirt
DESIGN FIRM Sayles Graphic Design
ART DIRECTOR John Sayles
DESIGNER John Sayles

All copy was hand rendered.

Event "Frontline"/Church Youth Event
Description of Piece(s) Poster,
collateral, jacket, flag
Design Firm Sayles Graphic Design
Art Director John Sayles
Designer John Sayles

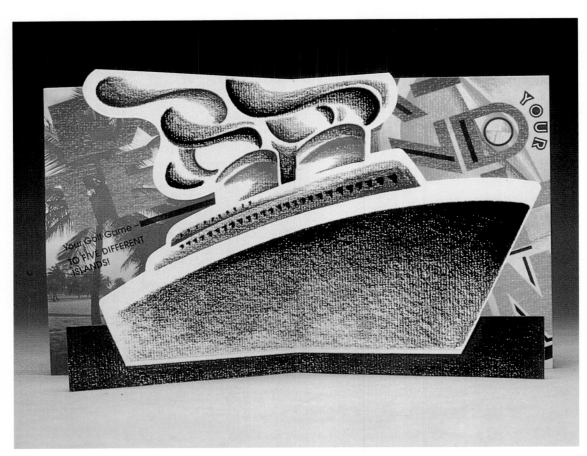

FACING PAGES

EVENT "EXPAND YOUR HORIZON"/CRUISE
    PROMOTION
DESCRIPTION OF PIECE(S) BROCHURE,
    POSTER
DESIGN FIRM SAYLES GRAPHIC DESIGN
ART DIRECTOR JOHN SAYLES
DESIGNER JOHN SAYLES

EVENT SPRING FLOWERS ADVERTISING
  CAMPAIGN/TOKYO DEPARTMENT STORE
DESCRIPTION OF PIECE(S) POSTERS
DESIGN FIRM MIKE QUON DESIGN OFFICE
ART DIRECTOR T. AONO
DESIGNER MIKE QUON
ILLUSTRATOR MIKE QUON

152

EVENT SUMMER SALE TOYS 'R' US
DESCRIPTION OF PIECE(S) POSTER
DESIGN FIRM CAMPBELL-EWALD
ILLUSTRATOR GARY CICCARELLI

INDEX

DIRECTORY

Adelle Bass & Co. Design
758 E. Colorado Boulevard #209
Pasadena, CA 91101

Al Perez Illustration & Design
175 East Olive Avenue
Suite 204
Burbank, CA 91502

Balcom Cantrell Advertising
Cotton Bowl Athletic Association
P.O. Box 569420
Dallas, TX 75356

Bartels & Company, Inc.
3284 Ivanhoe Avenue
St. Louis, MO 63139

Bennett/Ella
4527 Travis Street #200
Dallas, TX 75205

Bernhardt Fudyma Design Group
133 East 36th Street
New York, NY 10016

Bill Nelson Illustration Inc.
107 East Cary Street
Richmond, VA 23218

Boelts Bros. Design Inc.
14 East 2nd Street
Tucson, AZ 85705

The Bradford Lawton Design Group
719 Avenue E
San Antonio, TX 78215

Bruce Design
6660 Dixie Highway
Fairfield, OH

Carol Lasky Studio
30 The Fenway
Boston, MA 02215

Cato Design Inc.
254 Swan Street Richmond
3121 Victoria Australia

Catt Lyon Design Inc.
305 W. McMillan Avenue
Cincinnati, OH 45219

Chris Blakeman Design
819-1/2 W. Hays
Boise, ID 83702

Gary Ciccarelli
317 Elmwood
Dearborn, MI 48124

Clark/Thompson
19 West 21st Street
New York, NY 10010

C.O.W. Creative Operations Workshop
1606 Ponce de Leon Suite 502
Santurce, PR 00909

Creative Services/Titan Sports, Inc.
1241 E. Main Street
Stamford, CT 06902

Dale Vermeer Design
85 Hotel Street
Honolulu, HI 96813

Dan Frazier Design
1000 Jonell Lane
Chico, CA 95926

Daniels, Sid
12 East 22nd Street
Studio 11B
New York, NY 10010

Denver Nuggets
1635 Clay Street
Denver, CO 80204

Design Art, Inc.
6311 Romaine Street #7311
Los Angeles, CA 90038

DesignCentre of Cincinnati
225 East Sixth Street
Cincinnati, OH 45202

THE DESIGN COMPANY
79 KIRKLAND STREET
CAMBRIDGE, MA 02138

DILLON GRAPHICS
UNIT 4, 94 HAY STREET
SUBIACO, WESTERN AUSTRALIA 6008

DOREE LOSCHIAVO STUDIO
2714 S. MARVINE STREET
PHILADELPHIA, PA

DRENTTEL DOYLE PARTNERS
1123 BROADWAY
NEW YORK, NY 10010

THE DYNAMIC DUO, INC.
95 KINGS HIGHWAY SOUTH
WESTPORT, CT 06880

GARY HOUSTON DESIGN
1306 NW HOYT #203
PORTLAND, OR 97209

GOGOOP, INC.
532 KINSLEY AVENUE
4TH FLOOR
PROVIDENCE, RI 02909

THE GREEN HOUSE
64 HIGH STREET
HARROW ON THE HILL
MIDDLESEX HA1 3LL

GUGGENHEIM MUSEUM
575 BROADWAY 3RD FLOOR
NEW YORK, NY 10012

HAFFEMAN DESIGN GROUP INC.
935 W. CHESTNUT
SUITE 203
CHICAGO, IL 60622

HAPPYLIFE PRODUCTIONS
P.O. BOX 687
WOODSTOCK, NY 12498

HORNALL ANDERSON DESIGN WORKS
1008 WESTERN SUITE 600
SEATTLE, WA 98104

IMAGE GROUP
25 MAIN STREET
SUITE 203
CHICO, CA 95928

INTEGRATE, INC.
503 S. HIGH STREET
COLUMBUS, OH 43215

JIM LANGE DESIGN
203 N. WABASH #1312
CHICAGO, IL 60601

JINX STUDIO
27 W. 20TH STREET #1106
NEW YORK, NY 10011

LESLIE CHAN DESIGN CO., INC.
4F, 115 NANKING E. ROAD SEC 4
TAIPEI TAIWAN ROC

LINDA S. SHERMAN DESIGN, INC.
9825 CANAL ROAD
GAITHERSBURG, MD 20879

LISKA AND ASOCIATES, INC.
676 N. ST. CLAIR
SUITE 1550
CHICAGO, IL 60611

LYNNE CANNOY DESIGN
711 PENN AVENUE
SUITE 630
PITTSBURGH, PA 15222

MARK PALMER DESIGN
75-140 ST. CHARLES PLACE
PALM DESERT, CA 92211

MAY & CO.
3802 VINEYARD TRACE
MARIETTA, GA 30062

MENCHACA, RICHARD O.
106 MEREDITH
SAN ANTONIO, TX 78228

METROPOLIS, INC.
56 BROAD STREET
MILFORD, CT 06460

DIRECTORY

MIKE QUON DESIGN OFFICE
568 BROADWAY #703
NEW YORK, NY 10012

MODERN DOG
601 VALLEY STREET #309
SEATTLE, WA 98109

MULLER + COMPANY
4739 BELLEVIEW
KANSAS CITY, MO 64112

MYKLEBUST BROCKMAN INC.
3628 EAST AVENUE SOUTH
LA CROSSE, WI 54601

NANCY STUTMAN CALLIGRAPHICS
3008 RANA COURT
CARLSBAD, CA 92009

NEW IDEA DESIGN, INC.
3702 S. 16TH STREET
OMAHA, NE 68107

NEXTDOOR PRODUCTIONS
99-72 66TH ROAD
FOREST HILLS, NY 11374

NICEMAN
72 SPRING STREET
STUDIO 100
NEW YORK, NY 10012

NIKE, INC.
ONE BOWERMAN DRIVE
BEAVERTON, OR 97005

NORTH CAROLINA DANCE THEATRE
800 N. COLLEGE STREET
CHARLOTTE, NC 28202

NORTHERN ILLINOIS UNIVERSITY
OFFICE OF PUBLICATIONS
DEKALB, IL 60115

OSTRO DESIGN
147 FERN STREET
HARTFORD, CT 06105

PETER GOOD GRAPHIC DESIGN
3 NORTH MAIN STREET
CHESTER, CT 06412

THE PUSHPIN GROUP
215 PARK AVENUE SOUTH #1300
NEW YORK, NY 10003

RPM
JOHN D. SECKMAN JR.
779 8TH AVENUE
SAN FRANCISCO, CA 94118

RICKABAUGH GRAPHICS
384 WEST JOHNSTOWN ROAD
GAHANNA, OH 43230

SACKETT DESIGN ASSOCIATES
864 FOLSOM STREET
SAN FRANCISCO, CA 94107

SAYLES GRAPHIC DESIGN
308 EIGHTH STREET
DES MOINES, IA 50309

SCHWARTZ AND KAPLAN ADVERTISING
4649 PONCE DE LEON BOULEVARD
SUITE 301
CORAL GABLES, FL 33146

SEGURA INC.
361 W. CHESTNUT STREET
FIRST FLOOR
CHICAGO, IL 60610

SIMPSON DESIGN INC.
3700 CARLYLE CLOSE #905
MOBILE, AL 36609

SOMMESE DESIGN
481 GLENN ROAD
STATE COLLEGE, PA 16803

STAGEBILL
144 E. 44
NEW YORK, NY 10017

STEPHEN PERINGER ILLUSTRATION
17808 184TH AVENUE NE
WOODINVILLE, WA 98072

SULLIVANPERKINS
2811 MCKINNEY
SUITE 320, LB111
DALLAS, TX 75204

TAKAYUKI ITO DESIGN OFFICE
601, 9-2-13, AKASAKA
MINATO-KU
TOKYO 107 JAPAN

TARGET CENTER
600 1ST AVENUE NORTH
MINNEAPOLIS, MN 55403

THULE DESIGN
793 HIGUERA STREET #15
SAN LUIS OBISPO, CA 93401

TIRAPELLI DESIGN
215 MOFFETT PARK DRIVE
SUNNYVALE, CA 94089

TOKYU AGENCY INC.
4-0-18, AKASAKA
MINATO-KU
TOKYO JAPAN 107

TWO IN DESIGN
469 OAKDALE ROAD #9
ATLANTA, GA 30307

UNIVERSITY EVENTS OFFICE
UC SAN DIEGO
DEPT. 0078
9580 GILMAN DRIVE
LA JOLLE, CA 92093

VAUGHN WEDEEN CREATIVE
407 RIO GRANDE NW
ALBUQUERQUE, NM 87104

WRK DESIGN
02 WESTPORT ROAD
KANSAS CITY, MO 64111

WHITNEY EDWARDS DESIGN
3 NORTH HARRISON STREET
P.O. BOX 2425
EASTON, MD 21601

WILD HARE STUDIO
1601 ELKHORN AVENUE
BELLE FOURCHE, SD 57717

WINTERLAND PRODUCTIONS
100 HARRISON STREET
SAN FRANCISCO, CA 94105

THE WYANT GROUP, INC.
96 EAST AVENUE
NORWALK, CT 06857